MEL ALLWOOD

POCKET
MOUNTAIN BIKE
MAINTENANCE
REPAIRS ON THE ROAD

First published in 2005

10 9 8 7 6 5 4 3 2

Copyright © Carlton Books Limited 2005

A CIP catalogue record for this book is available from the British Library

ISBN 978-1-84442-245-6

Editor: Nigel Matheson
Design & project art direction: Darren Jordan
Production: Lisa French
Jacket & layout photography: Karl Adamson
Author photograph: J Kennedy

Printed and bound in Singapore

MEL ALLWOOD

POCKET
MOUNTAIN BIKE
MAINTENANCE
REPAIRS ON THE ROAD

CARLTON
BOOKS

Contents

Introduction

Mountain bikes

I became a cyclist originally because I live in a big crowded city and I'm an impatient traveller. Bikes are by far the quickest way to get around, and mean that I'm travelling under my own steam. I hate sitting in a tin box in traffic or waiting for unreliable public transport.

My first mountain bike was the key to discovering a whole new kind of cycling. Early adventures were mostly around the bridleways of the North Downs, a short train ride away from home, just outside London. Many mountain bikes, and great trips to fantastic remote places later, it's still one of my favourite places to ride. It doesn't have awesome scenery like Scotland or any classic epic loops like the Lakes, but it does have plenty of hidden trails, enough short sharp climbs to keep you fit, and lots of warm cosy pubs just when you need them. Everybody likes their own backyard best.

One of the attractions of mountainbiking for me is that it's a great way of getting to remote places, and you leave them behind pretty much as you found them. The peace comes at a price though – once you're off the beaten track, if anything goes wrong with your bike, you need to be able to rely on your own resources to fix it. So it pays to be familiar with your machine and carry basic tools and spares with you.

Like most bike mechanics, most of what I've learned about how to make bikes feel nice and work well comes from just taking things apart and putting them back together. I like fixing bicycles, which evolve, change and improve constantly, so that we all have to learn new tricks and techniques all the time. Bikes are relatively simple, and seldom need complex or expensive tools, but respond magically to a bit of care and attention – a

nurtured bicycle feels better than a neglected one that cost twice as much.

One of my favourite things about these bikes is that they have so few superfluous parts. Since you're the power source for this transport, you don't want to be carrying around anything you don't have to. But this positive can be a negative at the same time. Anything you break on a ride is probably vital, and must be repaired before you can continue.

Most bike repair careers start with trying to get home after something goes wrong. Even if this is as much as you ever intend to do with spanners, it's worth getting right – the difference between a glamorous repair story in the pub and a long dispiriting ride home is seldom more than a few basic tools and a bit of familiarity with the way your machine works.

It's a myth that some people have a special touch with mechanical things, a bit like having green fingers. The most vital quality you need to fix bikes is the ability to calmly assess the problem and work out a good solution. It's not magic – anyone can learn how to do this. Professional mechanics are just quicker at it and have more experience of similar problems.

Sometimes I worry that, one day, someone is going to force me to get a proper job, one that's neither as much fun nor involves using oily things. If that ever happens, a big chunk of what I've learned is in this book.

Mel Allwood, September 2005

Tools and Equipment

This section lists a basic toolkit, which you need to carry out regular maintenance and minor adjustments to your bike. It also contains a comprehensive toolkit, naming the tools you need to carry out the more involved repairs from the main chapters. It's worth investing in quality tools, which last longer and make any jobs you tackle easier. Also included is a list of useful spares – it's worthwhile having a few bits ready at home, in case you have an emergency when your bike shop is closed.

Multi-tools – compact and lightweight, with all the tools you'll need on the trail

The language of bicycle parts

People who talk about bikes sometimes sound like they're speaking a foreign language. Some of the words they use are unfathomable and bizarre, while some sound familiar but often mean something different to that expected. The language of bikes isn't just a way of keeping in the clique though – it's vital for identifying specific parts.

Disc brake callipers: (aka disc brake units) These are bolted to special disc mounts on your frame or fork. Operating the lever forces thin, hard pads onto your rotor, the metal disc attached to your hub. Powerful and lightweight, these can be daunting to service because they're new technology. However, they respond well to treatment with a few basic tools. Mechanical versions use normal V-brake levers and cables; hydraulic disc brakes use an oil-filled hose to force brake pads onto the rotor.

Cables and hoses: When connecting brake levers to callipers or V-brake units, these need to be kept in good condition to transmit an accurate signal. Speed control, as well as raw braking power, is vital. Steel cables run through lengths of outer casing from brake levers to V-brakes. Hoses are the stiff plastic tubes that transfer hydraulic brake fluid from hydraulic brake levers to callipers

Rear derailleur: This moves the chain step by step across the cassette sprockets. Different-sized sprockets give you different gear ratios so that you can pedal at a constant rate over a range of different speeds. The movement of the rear derailleur is controlled by a cable on the shifter on the right-hand side of the handlebar. Correct adjustment gives you slick shifting and ensures maximum life for your chain, chainset and cassette.

Chainset: This consists of three chainrings bolted together. Like the cassette sprockets, choosing a different size chainring gives you a different gear ratio. Larger chainrings give you a higher gear, which is harder to push but propels you further on each pedal stroke. Smaller chainrings give you a lower gear, allowing you to climb steep hills. Chainrings will wear out over time as the valleys between the teeth stretch until the chain slips under pressure.

Cassette and freehub: Your cassette consists of a set of different-sized sprockets bolted together. Currently nine-speed cassettes are most common and combine with the three chainrings on your chainset to give you 27 gears. Smaller cassette sprockets give you a higher (harder) gear for maximum speed, and larger sprockets give you a lower (easier) gear for climbing hills. The cassette is fitted to a freehub on your rear wheel.

Chain: The chain connects your chainset to your cassette so that when you pedal the back wheel goes around. It needs to be strong so it doesn't snap when you stand on your pedals and stamp up a hill, but it must also be flexible, so that it can shift from side to side across the cassette and chainset. Chain width needs to match your cassette: for example, nine-speed cassettes have narrower, more closely spaced sprockets than older eight-speeds so you need a narrower chain.

Headset: The main bearing at the front of your bike, the headset, connects your forks to your frame. This part is often ignored because it's mostly hidden in the frame. This bearing must be adjusted so it turns smoothly without rattling – any play or binding will affect your bike's handling. There are two types of headset: the newer "Aheadset" type shown here has almost completely superseded the older threaded headset. Regular servicing keeps bearings running smoothly and helps your headset last longer.

Bottom bracket: Bottom brackets are another "out-of-sight, out-of-mind" component. The bottom bracket axle connects your two cranks together through the frame. If worn and loose, the bottom bracket can lead to front gear shifting problems and cause your chain to wear out. Worn bottom brackets can be spotted by checking for side to side play in your cranks. Usually supplied as a sealed unit, this part must be replaced when worn or stiff. This repair needs a couple of specific but inexpensive tools.

Pedals: Introduced from road bikes, clipless pedals have replaced toe clips: a key-shaped cleat on the bottom of your shoe locks into a sprung mechanism on your pedals. The idea of clipless pedals is daunting for the first-timer, but you'll appreciate the extra power once you are used to them. Because your shoe is firmly attached, all your energy throughout the pedal stroke is used. Clean, oiled cleats will release your shoe instantly when you twist your foot. Many riders prefer flat pedals with studs.

Hubs: Well-adjusted hub bearings let wheels spin freely and save you energy. When properly adjusted, your bearings will be tight enough to prevent any side to side play without being so tight they slow you down. Occasional servicing to clean out any grit and dirt that has worked its way in will keep your wheels turning smoothly. Fresh, clean grease helps keep moisture out of your hubs. Jet-washing is tempting after a muddy ride, but will drive water in past your hub seals, flushing out the grease.

Suspension: Suspension makes your ride smoother. Almost all new mountain bikes come with front suspension forks, and full suspension bikes (with front suspension forks and a rear shock unit) get lighter and cheaper every year. Suspension bikes are better because they absorb trail shock and make you faster over uneven ground. The suspension keeps your centre of gravity moving forwards rather than up and down. Front forks and rear shocks need setting up for your weight and riding style.

Gearshifters

Seat post

Saddle

Rear derailleur hanger

Cassette

Disk brake calliper

Rotor

Valve

Tyre

Rim

Stem top cap

Stem

Headset

Suspension fork

Front hubs

Quick release

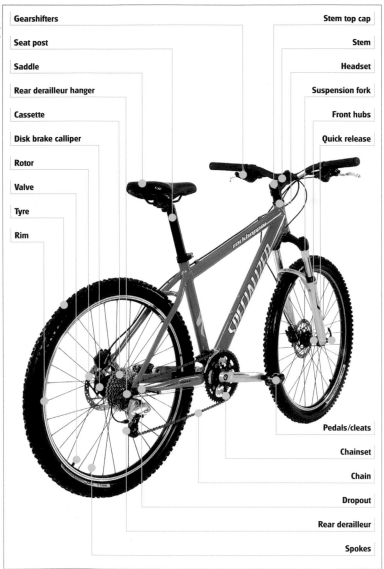

Pedals/cleats

Chainset

Chain

Dropout

Rear derailleur

Spokes

Tools and workshop equipment

Of course, everyone starts off with very basic equipment. Then gradually, as you get more confident fixing your bike, you find you need various other pieces of gear. Your toolkit grows and grows, until it reaches the happy point where you can tackle complicated tasks without investing in any more tools.

The evolving toolkit

Some tools are universal, like screwdrivers. Others are highly specific and only do one task, or even just one task on one particular make and model of component. When I was 18, I bought a socket to change the oil on my VW Beetle car. I sold the car a couple of years later, but the socket hung out in my toolbox until I didn't notice it any more. One day I cleared out my toolbox and realized I hadn't used it in 15 years – now it makes a nice candlestick on my bathtub. You can always find a new task for old tools so hang on to them.

The tools on the first list are good for a start and should allow you to carry out all the simple repairs you need. As your toolkit grows, a clear distinction will develop between your trail tools and your workshop tools. Trail tools need to be small and light and preferably foldable, so they don't stab you from inside a pocket when you fall off your bike. With workshop tools, the bigger and chunkier the better, first for proper leverage, and second so they last longer without wearing out. Neat and lightweight gadget tools will wear quickly if they get used frequently in the workshop.

Manuals and instructions are tools too

All new bikes and parts come with manuals or instructions. For some reason, it's traditional to throw them away without reading them. I don't know why. Don't do it.

Keep all instructions and manuals together: they're part of your toolkit. It is particularly important to keep the original

manual for suspension parts as fitting and setting-up instructions vary between make, model and year.

Once you find yourself using the manuals, feel free to scribble your own notes and diagrams on them as your knowledge grows.

The simple toolkit

When I started working on this section, I wrote and rewrote for the better part of a morning, adding and deleting items I believed were essential until, finally, I was happy with the result.

Then a friend came round, and together we calculated that the total cost of all the tools was more than her bike. I started again. The result is two lists: one of indispensable tools and a second for when you get more confident.

The second list is broken down to match chapters of the book, so you can buy items as you go along. Some tools are bike-specific. Some are obtainable from hardware or tool stores. Good tools last for years and are an investment. Cheap tools let you down when you least need it and can damage the component you're trying to fix. A plastic toolbox costs very little, and both keeps tools together and protects them from damage.

Don't lend your tools to anyone. This sounds harsh, but if you like someone enough to lend them a spanner, fix their bike for them instead. If you don't like them enough to fix their bike, you don't trust them enough to lend them your spanner.

The basic toolkit

The tools on this page are the indispensable ones you'll need to carry out the most basic repairs and maintenance on your bike.

- **Allen keys.** The best starter packs are fold-up sets of metric spanners (keys) that include 2, 2.5, 3, 4, 5 and 6mm sizes. You can use the body of the tool as a handle and bear down hard on it without bruising your hand. I'd rather choose a set with a wider range of keys than those you get that also come with screwdrivers, which are intended for trail use. Later, you will want separate Allen keys as they are actually easier to use. Those with a ball at one end allow you to get into awkward spaces.
- **A long-handled (about 200mm [8 inch]) 8mm or 10mm Allen key** is essential for most current crank bolts, which attach the pedals to the bottom bracket in the body of the bike. Older crank bolts take a 14mm socket.
- **Screwdrivers:** you'll need one flathead and one No.2 Phillips.
- **Metric spanners.** The 8, 9, 10, 15 and 17mm sizes are the most useful, but a metric spanner set that's got all the sizes from 8 to 17mm is ideal. The best are combination spanners, with a ring at one end (to grip all round the nut) and an open end at the other (easier to get into awkward spaces).
- **A big adjustable spanner,** also called a crescent spanner, with a 200mm-long [8 inch] handle is a good size to start with. The jaws must open to at least 32mm (1¼ inches). Always tighten the jaws firmly onto the flats of the nut before applying pressure to the handle to avoid damaging the nut and the jaws.

- **Good quality, bike-specific wirecutters** – not just pliers – can be purchased from your local bike shop. This tool can seem expensive, but both inner cable and outer casing must be cut neatly and cleanly.
- **Chain tool.** Again, quality really makes the difference. It's easy to damage an expensive chain with a cheap chain tool.
- **Chain-wear measuring tool.** An essential, this tool shows when your chain has stretched enough to damage other parts of the drivetrain.
- **A sharp knife with a retractable blade,** so you don't cut yourself digging in your toolbox for a spanner, is useful for cutting open packaging, releasing zipties (cable or electrical ties), etc.
- **A pair of pliers.**
- **A rubber or plastic mallet.** You can get these from hardware stores. A metal hammer is not a suitable alternative!
- **Puncture kit for standard and/or UST tubeless tyres.**
- **Track pump.** Frame-clipping pumps are intended for the trail, while a track pump gets plenty of air into the tires without you busting a gut. They're virtually essential for UST tubeless tires. Get one with its own pressure gauge, or buy a separate pressure gauge.

Sling a pen and notebook into your toolbox for making notes and drawing pictures as you take things apart.

It will help you reassemble them later. It's also useful for noting tyre pressures and suspension settings.

The comprehensive toolkit

As you develop a bit of expertise and start to tackle the major jobs, you have to add to your basic toolkit.

Brakes
If you use disc brakes, you need a bleed kit. You can either improvise one from tubes and bottles, or buy a specific one for your brakes. If you haven't bled brakes before, a kit makes it a lot easier. You should be able to tackle everything else with the basic toolkit.

A) Bottom bracket and headset
Headset spanners
You only need these for older, threaded headsets, which come in three sizes: 32mm (formerly standard), 36mm (called "oversize" but actually standard now) and 40mm (evolution size). Aheadsets are adjusted with Allen keys and don't need a spanner.

B) Bottom bracket tools
The most common style is the Shimano splined remover. This takes either a large adjustable spanner or a 32mm headset spanner. Remember, the right-hand side of the frame has a reverse thread. Facing the right-hand side of the bike, the righthand cup is removed clockwise. Facing the left-hand side, the left-hand cup is removed counterclockwise. Splined designs are wider than the older square taper ones; if you have an older version of the tool, the hole in the middle may not be big enough to fit over the splined axle. Sorry, you will just have to buy a new tool.

Transmission

- ◆ **Chain-cleaning box.**
- ◆ **Brush for chain cleaning.**
- ◆ **Crank extractor(s).** Essential for removing cranks and accessing the bottom bracket. You will need a spanner to drive the inner part of the extractor once the body is firmly screwed into the crank. The cranks are refitted using just the crank bolts – you don't need the extractor for this. There are two types of extractor: one for the newer splined axles, the other for the older square taper axles. An adapter allows you to use a square-type tool with splined axles, but splined tools will not fit square taper axles.

- ◆ **Cassette-remover and chain whip.** The cassette-remover fits into the splines at the centre of the cassette. You then need a big adjustable spanner to turn the tool. The chain whip fits around a sprocket and prevents the cassette turning as you undo its lockring. You don't need the chain whip for refitting the lockring; the ratchet in the middle of the cassette stops the cassette turning.
- ◆ **For freewheels** – how rear cogs were fitted on your wheel before cassettes were invented – you need the appropriate freewheel tool.

Chain-cleaning box

Cassette-remover

Crank extractors

Chain brush

Chain whip

Spoke spanner

Cone spanners

Wheels

- ◆ **Cone spanners.** These are for cup-and-cone bearings. Cone spanners are very thin so they can slot onto the narrow flats on the cones. Common sizes are 13, 15 and 17mm, but you'd best take your wheels to the bike shop and check the size before you buy.
- ◆ **Spoke spanner,** to fit your spokes. Take your wheels to the bike shop to check the size. Too small won't fit, too big will round off the nipple, which is really annoying.

Suspension
Shock tools

◆ These depend on the make and model of the shock. Check the owner's manual (which you have neatly filed!) for the tool list. If you have lost the manual, most are available on the net. Check the list of resources at the back of this book for common websites.

◆ **Air-sprung forks need a shock pump.** These have narrow barrels and accurate gauges to allow a precise volume of air into your shocks. If you buy a new air fork it may include a shock pump. You can also get tiny trail versions to fit in your pocket when you're out riding.

◆ **A small plastic measuring jug** for shock oil or a **plastic syringe.** They sell these in chemists for measuring out baby medicine.

Shock pump

Plastic syringe

Suspension fluid

Components
Pedal spanners

All makes of pedals except Time use a 15mm spanner. Pedal spanners are narrower than normal spanners so they can slot in between the pedal and crank, and are longer for extra leverage. Pedals must be fitted snugly or they work loose and rip out the crank threads. Some pedals use an Allen key, accessed from the back of the crank. For these you need a good-quality extra-long (200mm [8 inch]) Allen key or an extender bar.

Pedal spanner

Spare parts box

You need a box of spare parts as well. It's worth keeping bits and pieces in your house so you don't have to rush off in the middle of a job to pick them up.

◆ **Two tubes** the right size, with the correct valve for your wheels.
◆ **Brake blocks or pads.**

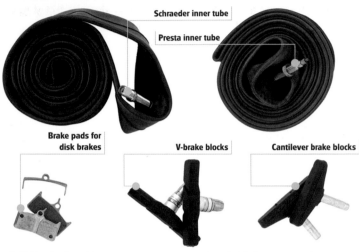

Schraeder inner tube

Presta inner tube

Brake pads for disk brakes

V-brake blocks

Cantilever brake blocks

◆ **A) Two brake cables.**
◆ **B) Two gear cables** and a length of gear outer casing.
◆ **C) Ferrules** (the end caps on casing) and end caps (the end caps on cables).
◆ **D) For Shimano chains:** chain-joining pins.
◆ **E) Zipties** (aka cable or electrical ties). These hold the fabric of the universe together. Before them we had string. Mountain biking couldn't exist until the ziptie was invented. Whoever

invented it deserves a major international prize. No toolbox should be without a few of them.
◆ **F) Electrical tape.**

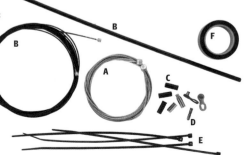

The biscuit box

One of the most irritating parts of bike repair is being thwarted by a simple task because you're missing a simple but very specific part. Bike shop workshops always have racks of plastic drawers full of tiny little parts, many of which are essential for just one job. This is a luxury you're unlikely to have at home.

Your tackle box is essential but, like a good compost heap, it must grow over time and cannot be bought wholesale! Start one now. A tackle box is any container into which you drop odd nuts and bolts left over from other bike repairs. When you shear off an essential bolt just after the stores have closed, your box of bits can save your bacon.

The box should be bike-specific – surplus woodscrews and outdated distributor caps don't count. Useful things include M5 (5mm diameter) bolts in lengths from 10mm to 45mm, crank bolts, Aheadset caps with rude slogans on them, odd washers, valve caps, ball bearings and scraps of chain.

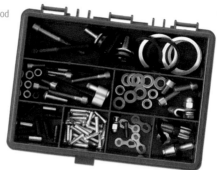

Your workshop

A proper workstand is probably your most expensive investment. Almost all the procedures listed in the main part of this book are easier if the bike is held steady with both wheels off the ground. Working standing up is easier than working crouched on the ground. A workstand also allows you to turn the pedals and wheels and observe everything working.

The next level down from a full workstand is a propstand, which keeps the back wheel off the ground and holds the bike upright.

If you have nothing, then improvise. Avoid turning the bike upside down – bikes don't like it. Instead, find an obedient friend who will hold the bike upright and off the ground at appropriate moments.

You need enough light to see by, especially for close-up jobs such as truing wheels. Most repairs are pretty messy. If you're working indoors, spread an old sheet on the floor before you start to catch things that drop and to protect the carpet. Ventilation is important. Any time you use solvents or spray, you need enough air circulating to dilute chemical fumes to harmless levels. Anything powerful enough to sweeten your bike will probably damage your body.

The same goes for bodily contact with substances. Consider wearing mechanics' rubber gloves. This saves loads of time cleaning your hands and reduces the quantity of chemicals absorbed through your skin. Lots of jobs involve removing something dirty, then either cleaning it or replacing it, before re-fitting it. You must have clean hands for the last part of the job – there's no point fitting a clean component with dirty hands.

Potions and lotions

A supply of cleaning and lubricating products is essential for routine maintenance. Your bike shop will usually have a choice. Ask for their recommendations, since they'll know what works well for your local environment. As you tackle more advanced jobs, you'll need some more specialized items.

Cleaning products

Always start with the least aggressive cleaning products, then gradually intensify.

- **A cleaning fluid,** for example Pedro's Bio Degreaser or Finish Line Bike Wash, both available in the US, or Muc-Off, available in the UK, makes washing quicker. Spray it on and leave it to soak in. In dry, dusty conditions you can wipe it off. Otherwise, rinse with clean water.
- **Degreaser.** This is great for cleaning up dirty drivetrains. Spray or paint it onto chain, front rings and cassettes; leave it to soak in; brush it off. Don't spray degreaser directly into wheel bearings, bottom brackets or headsets. It eats grease wherever it finds it, so if it does seep into bearings, you must strip them out and regrease them – a boring task. Also keep degreaser clear of suspension seals. Use a chain-cleaning box to keep the fluid contained.
- **Hand cleaner.** Essential! Most jobs start with a dirty procedure (like taking off an old broken part) and end with a clean one (such as adjusting a newly fitted part). Trying to assemble parts with new grease and dirty hands is a waste of time, so you need to be able to wash your hands in the middle of a job as well as at the end. Most hardware and car parts shops sell cleaner that's specially designed for oily hands. You'll also need plenty of cotton rags. The best source of this is often

charity shops. They usually have bags of T-shirts they can't sell as clothes, which make perfect rags. A sponge is better for paintwork than a brush.

Lubricant and grease

- **Chain lubricant.** This is an absolute essential. Everybody has a favourite type: with me it's Finish Line Cross-Country. Ask the mechanics in your local bike shop what they use. Different lubricants work in different climates. If you ride in a very wet and muddy place, you'll need a different lubricant from someone that rides in hot, dry climates. A dry climate requires a dry lubricant to keep the drivetrain running smoothly while attracting minimal muck. In muddy, wet conditions, you need a wet lubricant. These are stickier so they stay on in extreme conditions, but attract more dirt so you must be conscientious in your cleaning routine.

The important thing about chain lubricants is that they should be applied to clean chains. Putting oil on a dirty chain is the first step towards creating a sticky paste that eats expensive drivetrain components for breakfast. If you haven't got time to clean your chain first, you haven't got time to oil it. Whatever you use for oiling the chain will also do as a more general-purpose lubricant for cables, brake pivots, and derailleur pivots – anywhere two bits of metal need to move smoothly over each other.

I always use drip oil rather than spray oil. Spray is messy and wasteful, and it's too easy to get it on rims and disc rotors by mistake, which makes your brakes slippery rather than sticky. Your bike will be healthier if oil is delivered accurately to the places that need it the most.

◆ **Grease.** Confusion surrounds the difference between grease and oil. Essentially, they're both lubricants, but grease is solid and oil is liquid. Grease is stickier and can't be used on exposed parts of the bike; dirt sticks to the grease, forms a grinding paste and wears out the bike rather than making it run more smoothly. Grease is used inside sealed components like hubs. You don't get in there often so the stuff is required to last longer and remain cleaner. In an emergency almost any grease will do, but as you don't need much, get the good stuff from your local bike shop.

As your confidence grows, invest in a grease gun. This will keep your hands and grease stock clean.

For a clean and simple system, I like the ones that screw onto the top of a tube of grease. To get the last bit out, though, you usually abandon the gun and cut open the tube.

Specific lotions

As with your toolkit, start with a stock of essential items and build up as you tackle specialist jobs.

◆ **Disc brake fluid.** Use only the fluid specified for your brake system. DOT fluid, an autoparts trade standard, deteriorates once the bottle has been opened so buy in small amounts and open as you need it.

◆ **Suspension oil** is formulated to have damping properties. Its "weight" is critical and depends on the make and model of your fork or rear shock. Damping occurs by oil being forced through small holes. Lighter, thinner oil (e.g., 5wt) passes through more quickly. Heavier, thicker oil (e.g., 15wt) takes longer. Your fork or shock only works properly with the correct weight of oil: check the manual (which is, of course, neatly filed in your workshop!). You may mix two weights of oil to make an intermediate weight, but don't mix brands. See Chapter 7, for a full explanation.

◆ **Antiseize** (also called Ti-prep). This prevents reactive metals from sticking together and is especially important for titanium components, which react and seize whatever they touch. Avoid skin contact with antiseize; this stuff is not good for you.

◆ **Vaseline** is often the best substance for applying to seatposts in carbon frames. Check with the frame manufacturer's recommendations.

◆ **Plastic components.** These need their own lubricants. SRAM Twistshifter gear-changers and the Sachs equivalent, Twistgrips, have to be cleaned with a suitable degreaser (e.g., Finish Line Ecotech) or warm soapy water, and oiled with a special plastic lube (e.g., Jonnisnot).

◆ **Loctite glue.** The generic name is threadlock, although the Loctite brand is pretty good. Used where bolts cannot be allowed to rattle loose and between parts that may corrode together if moisture gets in, like rear hubs. Different colours indicate different strengths. Threadlock "#222" is red and is usually applicable up to M6 (6mm diameter) threads. Threadlock "#242", the most common, is blue and used for bolts M6 and above. Threadlock "#290", for holding pivot bushes, is green.

Rescue Repairs

Your routes may take you far off the beaten track into remote areas, where the ability to carry out basic maintenance will make you much more self-sufficient. Sometimes, a really simple repair can make the difference between a great ride, where you had to stop and fix your bike in the middle, and a really tedious day when you had to walk home from the furthest point. Once you've learned how to fix your own bike, you'll be able to fix other peoples' as well – and once they realize you're handy with your toolkit, they'll think twice before leaving you behind on a ride.

A rear derailleur by ESP technology

Rescue repairs for the trail: be self-sufficient on a bike

If you've never tackled the following jobs before, practise the following in the comfort of your own home: (1) getting the wheels on and off your bike; (2) removing and refitting tyres; and (3) splitting and rejoining chains. None of these repairs is difficult, but they're all much harder tackled the first time in the cold and wet.

Considering what we expect them to do, bicycles rarely go wrong. If you keep your bicycle well maintained, it will be unusual to face a trailside repair that is not on this list. However, you are occasionally faced with the unexpected. Once, miles from home with the night closing in, I had to make an emergency derailleur pivot. I succeeded, using a spare pivot from the dismantled innards of an Allen key tool held in place with a generous wad of electrical tape. The derailleur even changed gear quite effectively.

Keep your cool, be resourceful

Whenever you have to fix your bike by the side of the trail, think the task through carefully before you start.

If you're frustrated by a puncture or other repair, don't start fixing until you're less stressed. Do not, at any stage, throw your bicycle around, however petulant you feel. This improves nothing. You also look stupid.

Remember, everything you're carrying and wearing is a potential emergency spare part. Shoelaces, watchstraps, almost anything can be useful in ways you'd never think of until you really need them.

If you have to release your brakes to fix the bike, remember to refit them.

Spread a jacket out on the ground to catch pieces before you start work. Any part that falls off your bike or drops through cold, wet fingers can make a break for freedom, lying still and quiet in the grass until you've given up and gone away.

Your bicycle is on your side and really wants to get better, but it needs encouragement not abuse. Swear if you have to, but don't kick it.

Repairing your bike after a crash

The first priority after you've crashed is to assess yourself as safe to ride once the bike is fixed. I'm lousy at this. I always stand up as soon as possible and say things like "I'm fine," even if I can't remember who I am.

Don't believe it when anyone else puts on the act either. You may be shaken even if you're not injured. Stop and recover before you get back on the bike.

Once you've decided you are all right, check over the bike. Don't get sidetracked by obvious damage because there can often be more than one problem. Decide if you can safely repair the bike, or whether it will be quicker to walk out than struggle vainly for ages with the repair before limping home anyway.

Tools for the trail

Trail tools are things you carry around in the hope you never have to use them. When you ride with a group of people, it's worth being known as the person with a decent toolkit.

Even on a bad day when you are really slow, you will never get left behind.

Keep your trail tools completely separate instead of raiding your toolbox for them so you know everything is there. Replace anything you run out of right away – there's nothing more irritating than realizing your spare tube has a hole in it that you've been meaning to fix. Portable tools often aren't ideal for the workshop. Small, light spanners, for example, are great for the trail but are usually too flimsy for the workshop.

I use a seatpack. Lots of people carry their tools in a rucksack or bumbag, but they're heavy and painful to land on so I prefer to let the bike do the work. Seatpacks that clip on and off a clamp are best; it's annoying messing about with muddy Velcro straps on the trail. The following selection is a starting point rather than a definitive list. What you need still depends on your bike and riding environment. For example, the bolts on most bikes are the Allen key type, but if yours has nuts, you need the corresponding spanners. If you often get punctures – for example, because you ride thorny trails – carry extra tubes and patches.

Carry a patch kit even if you have a spare tube; punctures can come in batches. For long rides in remote places, you'll need to supplement this list. Ensure you know how to use what you're carrying! If you get desperate, you can stand by the side of the trail looking pathetic, hoping some kind soul who knows how to use your tools will ride past, but it's a risky strategy.

Trail tool pack

- **Spare tube** with the correct valve (thin Presta or fat car-type Schraeder) for your pump.
- **Pump.** Make sure it fits your inner-tube valves. Double-action pumps put air in as you both pull and push, refilling the tyre much more quickly. If you carry the pump on a bracket in your frame, use extra Velcro straps to ensure it doesn't rattle loose. After riding in muddy weather, clean the pump so the seals around the barrels stay airtight and won't leak. If you ride a lot in mud, carry the pump inside a backpack or bumbag to keep it clean. If the seals grit up and leak, the pump can't build up pressure.
- **Patch kit.** Once you've broken the seal on these, the glue dries out in about six months no matter how hard you screw on the lid, so make sure yours is fresh. UST tyres require a special type of patch kit; make sure you have the right one.
- **Tyre-levers.** If you're not confident about getting the tyre off the rim with two levers, then carry three – they don't weigh much. Plastic levers are far better than metal ones, which damage the rims.
- **Allen key/screwdriver fold-up toolset.** I prefer the fold-up tools for trail use: they're easier to find if you drop them, and the body of the tool makes a comfortable handle for tightening and loosening bolts without hurting your hand. As a bare minimum, you need 4, 5 and 6mm Allen keys, a flathead screwdriver and a Phillips screwdriver.
- **Chain tool.** For Shimano chains you also need to carry appropriate spare rivets. You can also buy spare Powerlinks (see Split Links later in this chapter), which are a quick and easy way to split and rejoin chains, and weigh almost nothing.
- **Zipties.** These are essential for emergencies and come out top in the weight-to-usefulness chart.
- **A strip of duct tape,** wrapped around the barrel of your pump. Like zipties, it weighs almost nothing and can come in very handy in an emergency.

Punctures

Punctures are inevitable. The pressure inside the tyre is higher than the pressure outside, and the world is full of sharp things. Don't worry if you've never fixed a flat before though; it's not as difficult as people make out. And, like learning to tie your shoelaces, it gets easier with practice.

There are ways to reduce the number of punctures you get. Occasionally you pick up a sharp object that cuts straight through tyre and tube and causes a flat, but often objects take a while to work their way through the casing of the tyre. Before you set out, check both tyres: raise each wheel off the ground in turn, spin each slowly, and pick out foreign objects. Maximum and minimum pressures are printed or stamped on the tyre sidewall. Make sure the tyre is inflated to at least the minimum suggested pressure to reduce the chance of snakebite flats (caused when pressure from, say, a rock edge, squeezes two symmetrical holes in the tube against the sides of the rim). If you like riding at very low pressure, choose a tyre designed to take it. These tyres have a thicker sidewall, which

won't fold over itself and pinch the tube.

Problems with punctures at, or around, the valve can also be caused by low tyre pressures. If there isn't enough air in it, the tyre will creep gradually around the rim, dragging the tube with it. The valve is held in place in the valve hole, so the tube around it becomes stretched and tears easily, ripping the valve out of the tube. Check your tyres regularly for large cuts as well – under pressure the tube will bulge out of these cuts and burst instantly. Some people suffer from punctures more than others. If you feel unfairly cursed, consider investing in puncture-resistant tyres. These have an extra layer of tough material incorporated into the carcass of the tyre under the tread, which helps to stop sharp things working their way through.

REPLACING TUBES

◀ **Step 1:** If you have rim brakes, you need to release them to get the tyre out easily. For V-brakes, pull the black rubber boot off the end of the noodle, squeeze the brake units together, and pull the noodle out and then up to release it from its nest. For cantilever brakes, squeeze the brake units together and push the cable nipple down and out of the slot in the unit.

◀ **Step 2:** Turn the bicycle upside down. Undo quick-release skewer. Unless you have a fancy skewer set, do this by folding (not turning) the handle over the axle. If you're unsure how to use quick-releases safely, read the section on them before you go any further (page 51). For the front wheel, undo the nut on the opposite side of the wheel several turns to get past the dropout tabs.

◀ **Step 3:** The rear wheel is a little trickier to remove than the front. Stand behind the bike. With your left hand, pull the body of the derailleur backwards with your fingers, and push the cage forwards with your thumb, as shown. This creates a clear path, so that you can lift the rear wheel up and forwards, without getting tangled up in the chain.

◀ **Step 4:** Inspect the outside of the tyre before you go any further to see if you can work out what caused the puncture. There may be nothing – you may have had a snakebite puncture or the escaping air may have ejected whatever caused the puncture. If you find something sharp, pry it out.

◀ **Step 5:** If there's any air left in the tyre, expel it. Remove the valve cap. For Presta valves (long and thin), undo the little thumb nut on top of the valve and press it down. For Schraeder valves (short, fat, car-tyre type), use something sharp, like a key, to push down the pin in the middle of the valve. The more air you get out of the tube at this stage, the easier it is to get the tyre off.

◀ **Step 6:** Each side of the tyre is held on by an internal wire, or Kevlar hoop, called the bead. To remove the tyre, lift enough of the bead over the sidewall of the rim. With care, this can be done by hand. Hold the wheel upright facing you. Work around the tyre, pushing the side closest to you into the dip in the middle of the rim. This will give you enough slack to pull the bead off.

◀ **Step 7:** With the wheel still upright and facing you, pinch a 10cm (4 inch) section of the side of the tyre nearest you with both hands. Lift this section up and over the rim, towards you. Hold it in place with one hand, and work gradually around the tyre with the other, easing the bead over the rim. Once you've got about a third of the tyre off, the rest will come away easily.

◀ **Step 8:** If you can't get the tyre off by hand, you need to use tyre-levers. Starting opposite the valve, tuck one lever under the bead in line with the spokes. Fold it back and hook the lever under the spoke to hold it in place. Move along two spokes and repeat with a second lever, then repeat with a third lever. Remove middle lever, leapfrog one of the others and repeat.

◀ **Step 9:** If the valve has a little nut screwing it to the rim, undo it. Reach inside the tyre and pull out the tube. Leave the other side of the tyre in place.

Toolbox

- **Spare tube** – check that the valve matches the tubes on your bike
- **Puncture kit** – backup in case you get more than one puncture
- **Pump** – make sure it works on your valve type. A pressure gauge is useful
- **Tyre-levers** – two is standard, take three if you're not confident
- **Spanners** – any spanners you need to remove your wheels
- **Tool pack** – carry these separately, so you can find them quickly
- **Warm clothes** – a hat to put on to keep you warm while you fix your bike – I get cold very quickly as soon as I stop riding

Refitting a new tube

It's vital to work out what caused the puncture before you fit a new tube. If the problem's still there when you fit a new tube, you'll puncture again right away – which is even more irritating if you haven't got a second spare tube.

Your first step is to inspect the tyre carefully. Look around the outside for thorns, shards of glass or sharp stones. If you can't see anything from the outside, check the inside of the tyre too. The easiest way to locate the culprit is to feel around inside the tyre with your fingers, moving slowly and carefully to avoid cutting yourself. If you're still unsure what caused the flat, pump air into the tube and locate the hole. You may be able to hear it rushing out of a big hole. Smaller holes can be harder to find – pass the tube slowly through your hands so that you can feel the air on your skin. You can put the tube in a bowl of water and watch for bubbles, but I don't usually carry a bowl of water in my emergency toolkit. Sometimes you can use puddles as an alternative. Once you've found the hole in the tube, hold the tube up to the tyre to locate the area of the tyre where the puncture occurred, and inspect the tyre again carefully.

Remove anything that you find. You won't necessarily find something in the tyre because punctures happen in other ways too. Pinch punctures – also known as snakebite flats – happen when you don't have enough tyre pressure. If you hit a rock hard the tyre squashes, trapping the tube between the rock and your rim. Pinch flats are usually easy to identify: you have two neat holes in your tyre, a rim width apart. Check the tyre sidewalls as well because a hole here will turn into a fresh puncture immediately. Big tears or gashes in the tyre will need to be repaired before you fit a new tube. Duct tape is ideal for smaller holes.

FITTING THE NEW TUBE

◀ **Step 1:** Now for the new tube. Remove the nut on the valve, if there is one. Pump a little air into the tube – just enough to give it shape. This will prevent the tube getting trapped under the bead as you refit the tyre. Pull back the section of tyre over the valve hole and pop the valve through the hole. Work around the tyre, tucking the tube up inside it.

◀ **Step 2:** Returning to the opposite side of the valve, gently fold the tyre back over the rim. This gets tougher as you go. When there's just a short section left, you'll get stuck. Push the sections of tyre you've already fitted away from the sidewall of the rim and into the dip in the middle, like you did to get it off. You should then be able to ease the last section on with your thumbs.

◀ **Step 3:** If you can't hand-fit the last section, use tyre-levers. Work on short sections 5cm (2 inches) at a time. Take care not to trap the tube between the rim and the tyre-lever as it's easy to pinch-puncture it. Once the tyre is reseated, push the valve up into the rim so that it almost disappears (to make sure the area of tube near the valve is not caught under the tyre bead).

◀ **Step 4:** Pump up the tyre. If you had a snakebite flat last time, put in a little more air. Once the tyre is up, retighten the thumb nut on Presta valves, screw the stem nut back onto the valve stem, and refit the dustcap. Don't fit the valve stem nut until the tube is inflated, as you risk trapping a bulge of the tube under the tyre bead.

◀ **Step 5:** Rear wheel: with the bike upside down, stand behind it and hold wheel in your right hand. Put a left-hand finger in front of the guide jockey wheel (nearer the ground in this position), and your thumb behind the tension jockey wheel. Pull finger back and push thumb forwards, then place wheel so sprockets are within the loop of the chain. Guide the axle into the dropouts and secure.

◀ **Step 6:** Refit the front wheel. This is easier. Drop the wheel into the dropout slots; make sure there's an equal amount of space between the tyre and the fork legs, and tighten the quick-release lever securely.

◀ **Step 7:** For disc brakes, wiggle the rotor (A) into place between the brake pads before settling the wheel into the dropout slots. You need to check that the rotor is sitting centrally between the brake pads inside the calliper. If it's hard to see, hold something light-coloured on the far side of the calliper. You may need to adjust the position of the wheel slightly so that the rotor is central.

◀ **Step 8:** For rim brakes, don't forget to refit the brakes – it's easy to overlook this vital stage in the excitement of fixing your puncture. Pull the brake units together and refit the cable. If you have V-brakes take care to seat the end of the noodle (B) securely in the key-shaped nest.

◀ **Step 9:** Turn the bike back over and check that the brakes work: pull the front brake on and push the bike forwards. The front wheel should lock and the back one should lift off the ground. Pull the back brake on and push the bike forwards. The back wheel should lock, sliding across the ground. Lift up the wheels and spin them. Check that rim brakes don't rub on tyre.

Checklist: what caused the puncture?

- Sharp things (thorns, glass, flint) cutting through the tyre
- Cuts or gashes in the tyre that allow the tube to bulge out – check both the sidewall and the tread
- Snakebite punctures – when the tyre, without enough air, gets trapped between the rim and a rock
- Rim tape failure – when sharp spoke ends puncture the tube or when the tube gets trapped in rim holes
- Valve failure – when under-inflated tyres shift around on the rim
- Badly adjusted rim brakes – when blocks are set too high

Stiff links/split links

You feel a stiff link as you're riding along – the pedals slip forwards regularly, but at different places in the pedal revolution.

To find a stiff link, change into the smallest sprocket at the back and the largest chainring at the front. Lean the bike up against a wall and pedal backwards slowly with your right hand. The chain heads backwards from the top of the front chainring, around the smallest sprocket, around the front of the guide jockey and the back of the tension jockey. Then it heads to the

front chainring again. The chain is straight as it travels across the top, then bends around the sprocket. The links should be flexible enough to straighten as they emerge from the bottom of the sprocket, then bend the other way to pass round the guide jockey. A stiff link won't straighten out as it drops off the bottom of the cassette and passes clumsily around the derailleur.

REPLACING STIFF LINKS

◀ **Step 1:** Once you've identified the problem link, get your chain tool out. You need to use the set of supports nearest the handle – the spreading supports. Look carefully at the problem rivet to identify whether one side of the rivet sticks further out one side of the chain than the other. If it is uneven, start with the sticking-out side. If it looks even, start with either side.

◀ **Step 2:** Lay the chain over the supports and turn the handle clockwise until the pin of the chain tool almost touches the rivet on the chain. Wiggle the chain to precisely line up the pin with the rivet. Turn until you can feel the pin touching the rivet, then just a third of a turn more. Back off the tool and wiggle it to see if the link is still stiff. Repeat if necessary.

◄ Step 3: If you don't have the chain tool with you, hold the chain as shown and flex it firmly backwards and forwards between your hands. Stop and check frequently to see if you've removed the stiff link. The last thing you want is to go too far and twist the chain plates.

Split links

A split link, also called Powerlink, is a quick and easy way to split and rejoin chains. It is particularly useful if you like to remove your chain to clean it, since repeatedly removing and replacing the rivets in chains can cause weak spots. It's also a great emergency fix.

◄ Powerlink – the quick and easy way to split and rejoin chains

You still need your chain tool for removing the remains of twisted or broken links, but the split link will not be stiff when you refit it and does not shorten the chain.

There are a couple of different types of split links; the best is the Powerlink, which comes free with SRAM chains. All split links work in similar ways.

The link comes in identical halves, each half with one rivet and one key-shaped hole. To fit, you pass a rivet through each end of the chain, linking the ends together through the wide part of the hole. When you put pressure on the chain it pulls apart slightly and locks into place. They never release accidentally.

To split the chain, locate the split link and push the adjacent links towards each other. The Powerlink halves are pushed together, lining up the heads of the rivets with the exit holes. You can then push the two halves across each other to release them.

Fixing a broken chain

After punctures, repairing a chain is the most common trailside task. Chains get damaged by rocks and pebbles flicking up and trapping between chain and sprocket (gear ring). A mistimed or clumsy shift of the gears can have the same effect, putting pressure on the chain when it's stretched. Old, worn and neglected chains develop weak spots over time and are more likely to let you down under pressure.

For any kind of chain problem you'll need a chain tool. These are annoying to carry because they only do one job. But when you have a broken chain nothing else will do – if you haven't got one, you're walking home. It can be shocking when a chain breaks – one moment you're stamping hard on the pedals, the next moment all resistance is gone and you're left with spinning feet and no balance.

Your first step is to go back and retrieve the chain. They usually unroll in a straight line in the direction you were travelling, so if your chain is not immediately obvious, walk back parallel to the way you came and check your path. If you were moving fast it may be some way back.

Checking a repaired chain

Once you've finished rejoining the broken parts it's important to check that the repaired chain is still long enough to reach all the way around your drivetrain. It will be slightly shorter, since you will have removed damaged links. It is essential that there is still enough slack in the chain even in the largest sprocket, so that the derailleur is not strained or twisted. Otherwise, you risk tearing the derailleur off, damaging both the derailleur and the part of the frame to which it attaches.

Get someone to lift up the back of the bike for you, then change into the smallest sprocket at the back and the largest chainring at the front – pedal with your left hand and change gears with your right. Then change gears click by click towards the largest sprocket at the back, while watching the derailleur. As you move into larger sprockets, the derailleur will get stretched forwards. Check the tension of the lower section of the chain where it passes from the bottom of the chainring to the rear derailleur. If this section becomes tight, stop shifting. If you force the chain into a larger sprocket once the chain is tight, you'll damage the derailleur.

If the derailleur is struggling to reach the largest sprocket at the back, it's important not to change into this gear as you ride along.

Try to remember not to use this gear. Personally, I prefer to readjust the end-stop screw on the rear derailleur so that I cannot accidentally change into the largest chainring, because it's all too easy to forget once you start riding.

Shift click by click into larger gears until the chain becomes taut, then screw in the "low" end-stop screw until you can feel resistance – it will touch the tab inside the derailleur that limits further movement.

Once you get home, replace the chain with a new, longer one (you'll almost certainly need a new cassette too) and readjust your end-stop screw, so that the chain reaches the largest sprocket.

MENDING A CHAIN

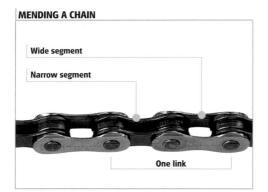

Wide segment

Narrow segment

One link

◀ **Step 1:** Once you have the chain, look at both ends. One will be a narrow segment of chain and the other a wide segment. A complete link consists of one wide and one narrow segment. You will usually find that the plates on the wide segment got twisted and damaged as the chain broke, so this complete link (the damaged wide one plus the narrow one adjacent to it) has to be removed.

◀ **Step 2:** Look carefully at the chain to choose the right place to break it. When you come to rejoin it, you need to match up a narrow and a wide segment. Once you've selected the correct rivet, lay the chain over the chain tool as shown. Your chain tool probably has two sets of supports to lay the chain over. Choose the set furthest from the handle of the tool.

◀ **Step 3:** Turn the handle of the tool clockwise, so that the pin approaches the chain. When you get close, line up the pin very carefully with the centre of the chain rivet. If the pin is not properly aligned with the rivet you risk damaging the chain plates – creating a new weak spot on your chain – as you push the rivet out.

◀ Step 4: As you rotate the handle of the chain tool it will start to push the rivet out of the chain. Be careful how far you push the rivet through. If the chain is a Shimano – and you have a replacement rivet – push the old rivet all the way out. However, with other makes of chain you reuse the original rivet and must make sure you don't push it out completely because they're awkward to replace.

◀ Step 5: Ideally, you need to stop pushing the rivet when there's a little stub poking out just this side of the outer plate, well before it falls out. With a Park tool, wind the handle in until it won't go any further – this is exactly the right amount. You'll have to flex the chain slightly, as shown, to free the inner segment from the stub of rivet sticking out, then separate the chain.

One link

◀ Step 6: You'll have to take out a complete link – one wide section and one narrow section – so repeat the process, two rivets along, on the other side of your twisted link. You should now have a broken link and a slightly shortened chain; one end should end in a wide segment, the other in a narrow segment. Turn it so that the rivet at the wide end faces towards you.

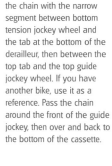

◄ Step 7: Feed the end of the chain with the narrow segment between bottom tension jockey wheel and the tab at the bottom of the derailleur, then between the top tab and the top guide jockey wheel. If you have another bike, use it as a reference. Pass the chain around the front of the guide jockey, then over and back to the bottom of the cassette.

◄ Step 8: Continue behind the bottom of the cassette, up and forwards over the top and then towards the chainset. Pass the chain through the front derailleur. It will eventually have to sit on the chainrings but, for now, pass it around the front of the chainset, then drop it into the gap between the chainset and the frame to give yourself enough slack to rejoin the chain easily.

◄ Step 9: If you're refitting a standard chain, ease the two ends together, flexing the chain so you can slide the inner segment of chain past the stub of rivet sticking through to the inside of the outer plates. Once you've got it, though, the stub will make it easy to locate the rivet in the hole in the inner plates, lining the two ends of the chain up.

◀ **Step 10:** Lay the chain over the chain support furthest away from you. Turn the handle clockwise until the pin on the chain tool almost touches the rivet on the chain. Wiggle the chain to precisely line up the pin with the rivet.

◀ **Step 11:** Keep turning the handle, while pushing the rivet into the chain, until there is an even amount of rivet showing on both sides of the chain. Remove the tool.

◀ **Step 12:** Rejoining the chain usually squashes the plates together and makes the link stiff – see page 34 to remedy. Finally, reach around behind the chainset and lift the chain back onto a chainring. Stand up, lift the saddle up with your left hand and push the pedal around with your right foot so that the chain can find a gear.

Shimano chains

Shimano chains need to be treated slightly different from standard chains. The rivets that join each link are very tightly fitted together, so it will usually damage the chain plates if you try to reuse an original one.

When splitting and rejoining a Shimano chain the rivet must be pushed all the way out, then it has to be replaced with a special Shimano joining rivet.

The rivets are different lengths to match the different chain widths used by eight- and nine-speed systems, so make sure to choose the correct replacement: the longer eight-speed rivets are grey, the shorter nine-speed version is silver.

The replacement rivet is twice as long as the original rivets and has a groove in the middle. The first section is a guide to locate the rivet correctly in the chain and must be broken off once the second part of the rivet has been driven home with the chain tool. This means you need pliers to snap the guide off, as well as a replacement rivet.

Shimano chains are not designed to be used with Powerlinks, Superlinks or similar – they must only be fixed by replacing a rivet that has been removed with the special Shimano joining pin.

If you look carefully, you will see that each of the wider chain links is carefully shaped, with a bulge at either side.

These help the chain to lift easily onto a new sprocket when changing gear at the back, and a new chainring when changing gear at the front.

As with other brands, don't be tempted to patch together a chain with scraps from other makes – or to add new bits of chain into an old chain to make it longer. This will not work for one simple reason: the mismatched sections won't mesh properly with your sprockets, causing excessive chainwear and possible chainsuck.

REFITTING A SHIMANO CHAIN

◀ **Step 1:** Push the ends together until the holes line up, then push through the replacement rivet. The first half of the rivet goes through easily, holding things together while you use the chain tool. Lay the chain on the furthest supports of the chain tool, and turn the handle of the tool clockwise until the second half of the rivet begins to emerge.

41

◄ Step 2: Snap off the section of rivet sticking out, ideally with pliers. If you don't have any, trap the end of the rivet between two Allen keys on a multitool and twist.

◄ Step 3: Wriggle the new link. Often it is stiff because the plates get stuck together. Lay the chain back over the chain tool with the stiff rivet in the set of supports nearest the handle. Wind the handle in until the pin touches the rivet, then a further third of a turn to loosen link. Reach in behind chainset and lift chain back onto a chainring.

Successful chain-fixing – key points to note

- Always use a good-quality chain tool. Modern chains are made so the rivet is a very tight fit in the chain plate This helps to stop you from breaking them, but means that they will laugh at anything less than a proper chain tool.
- Big multi-tools sometimes include a chain tool. These are always better than nothing, but seldom as good as a proper separate one.
- Align the pin of the chain tool very carefully with the centre of the rivet, otherwise you risk damaging the chain plates and mangling the link.
- Always check links that you've just joined. They'll often be stiff because the chain plates get squashed together as you push the rivet through them. See page 34 to remedy.

Shortening chain to singlespeed

If you destroy your rear derailleur in a crash you are forced to run your chain on a single sprocket because you can no longer change gear. This repair tends to be more successful on hardtails (suspension forks only) than on full-suspension bikes, depending on how much of an effect the movement of the suspension has on the length of the chain. If you have to shorten the chain on a full-suspension bike you have to measure the length of the chain that you need with the suspension at its full extension.

The first task is choosing a suitable gear. The one with the best chance of success is the middle chainring at the front and the smallest sprocket at the back. Choose a random place in the chain and use the chain tool to split the chain, as shown on page 31. Remember to leave a stub of rivet sticking out to locate the hole in the rejoined chain later. Separate the two ends.

Unthread the chain from the rear derailleur and reroute it to pass through the front derailleur around the chainring of choice, back around a sprocket on the cassette while bypassing the rear derailleur altogether, and then forwards to meet up with the other end of the chain. Match up the ends and choose

where you're going to shorten the chain. Finding the perfect spot is sometimes tricky, but it's better to end up with a slightly slack chain than one that is too tight and binding. A binding chain will probably just break again.

Rejoin the chain, using the instructions on page 36. You have to ride carefully to keep the shortened chain in place without the tension from the rear derailleur, a component you don't notice until it's gone. Keep up an even pedalling pressure and don't be tempted to stand up on the pedals, because the extra jerkiness often throws the chain off.

Remember to save the section of chain you had to remove – you'll need to reuse it once you've repaired or replaced your derailleur. Chains and cassettes wear into each other with the chain stretching at the same rate the teeth wear, widening the valleys between teeth. You cannot just replace a chain, or a section of it, with a new chain without replacing your cassette at the same time. Your new chain will just skip and slip on the old cassette.

◀ **Route the chain around the smallest sprocket, bypassing the rear derailleur**

Crank and pedal repairs

Every time you stand up on your pedals to haul yourself up the last steep bit of a hill, or you change into your biggest gear and sprint madly to beat your friends back to the car, you're relying on your cranks and pedals to stay firmly bolted onto your bike. Mostly they do the job, but sometimes they let you down.

The most common problem is crank bolts working loose and falling out, so that your crank drops off next time you lean on it. This is almost always a left-hand crank problem. Crank bolts are both normal threads that tighten clockwise.

As you pedal forwards the surface of each crank will rub on the underside of a loose crank bolt. This will tend to tighten a right-hand crank and loosen a left-hand crank. Once the left-hand side starts to work its way free every pedal stroke will make it a little looser.

Of course, this won't happen if you tighten the crank bolt firmly when you fit it and check it regularly, but this kind of clever hindsight is a bit useless when your crank falls off in the middle of nowhere. It's also particularly unhelpful for anyone else at this point to ask you whether you'd checked the bolt regularly.

Don't hit the speaker though: smug people who ask questions like this when your bike breaks often carry useful tools you might need to borrow.

Once your crank has fallen off or come loose you have several options. If you still have the bolt you're in business – retighten it firmly. Multi-tools often have the most common 8mm Allen key size but are far too short to apply enough pressure for a permanent repair.

Wrap gloves or fabric of some kind around the tool, so that you can apply as much force as possible. Standing with one foot on the tool and the other on the pedal often works well, but you'll have to find something to lean the bike against while you are performing this task. Most importantly, stop frequently to retighten the crank bolt – at least every twenty minutes.

If you can't manage to find the bolt your simplest option is to remove the crank completely, balance your left foot on the side of the bottom bracket, and pedal with your right foot.

This is an easier task than you might expect, but is surprisingly hard work going uphill when you'll be better off walking. This is least unpleasant if you have clipless pedals.

Securing your crank

If you have a way to go to get home a little bit of time spent securing your crank will pay off. Even if you can't find the original bolt you still have a spare – it's holding your other crank on.

Remove the right-hand crank bolt and use this to tighten your left-hand cranks as firmly as possible onto the axle. Remove it again and refit it back onto the right-hand crank. Chainsets are more expensive than cranks and so are not worth sacrificing.

An emergency crank bolt will help keep the crank in place. If you can, carve a short stub out of a handy-sized branch, then screw it into the end of the axle. Cut off any wood that protrudes out of the crank though – it will be in just the right position to take chunks out of your ankle. Pedal gingerly!

Emergency wheel repairs

Wheels are excellent at resisting forces that are in line with them, like supporting your weight riding or jumping. However, they buckle easily under forces from the side, the kind of forces that are common when you crash.

A common disaster is crashing and folding either wheel so badly it won't turn between the brake blocks. The temptation is to release the offending brake and carry on riding, but clearly this is a bad idea – you're careful for 10 minutes, then you forget you only have one brake and pick up speed. And suddenly you've crashed again.

Use these pages to straighten your wheel by adjusting the tension in your spokes.

Your rim is supported all the way around by the tension in your spokes. The tension in each spoke can be increased or reduced by tightening (counterclockwise) **(A)** or loosening (clockwise) **(C)** the spoke nipple, effecting the short section of the rim to which the spoke is attached. Alternate spokes are attached to opposite sides of the hub. Tightening a spoke that leads towards the right-hand side of the hub will move the rim towards the right **(B)**; loosening this spoke will allow the rim to move towards the left. Truing wheels is about adjusting the tension in each spoke, so that the rim runs straight with no side-to-side wobble. This process is not the magic art that it's often made out to be – as long as you're careful about three things:

1) Spend a little time choosing the right spokes to adjust. Spin the wheel and watch the rim. Identify the section of the rim that is most bent – you may be lucky and have one single bent zone that you can concentrate on, but if the wheel is really buckled you will have to estimate where the centreline should be.

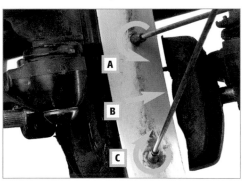

2) Working out in which direction to turn each spoke nipple is really tricky at first. Use the photo (left) as a guide. Watch the rim as you turn the nipple. If the bulge gets worse rather than better you're turning the nipple the wrong way.

3) Adjust the tension in each spoke in tiny steps. It's much better to work a quarter of a turn of the nipple at a time. Cranking the spoke key around in whole turns is a recipe for disaster. Adjust a quarter-turn, check the effect that you've had on the rim, go back and repeat if necessary.

Broken spokes

If you ride a wheel with a spoke missing, and don't straighten it, you will bend the rim permanently. Yet, as only long-distance riders heading for the Himalayas ever seem to carry spare spokes, there's a limit to what you can do if one does break. Rear wheel spokes can't be replaced unless you have the tools to remove and refit the cassette, making an emergency fix unlikely. But you can adjust the surrounding spokes to make the wheel as straight as possible, getting your brakes to work better (if you have rim brakes), and making it more likely you will be able to fix the wheel properly later.

First, render the snapped spoke safe by preventing it from wrapping around anything else. If it's broken near the rim, wind it around an adjacent spoke to keep it from rattling around. If it's broken near the hub, bend it in the middle so that you can hold it still. Use a spoke key to unwind the nipple so that the spoke drops out of the end of the nipple. If it's broken in the middle, which is the least likely, do both.

Lift up the wheel and spin it gently to see how bent it is. There will usually be a single large bulge where the spoke is broken. Use a spoke key to loosen the spokes on either side of the missing one. It can be confusing working out which way to turn. Look at the spoke you want to turn and imagine you can see the top of the spoke nipple through the tyre. To loosen a spoke, turn it so that the top of the spoke head turns counterclockwise.

With rim brakes, check the clearance between brake blocks and tyre. You may find that the tyre rubs on the brake block in the broken spoke zone. If this is the case, loosen

the Allen key bolt that holds the brake block in place, and move the block down slightly so that it clears the tyre. Retighten securely.

Straightening a bent wheel

With a spoke key you can sometimes get the wheel straight enough to ride safely. As a guideline, if the wheel has more than 2cm (1 inch) of sideways movement when you spin it, you are unlikely to be able to straighten it with a spoke key. One seldom appreciated advantage of disc brakes is that the brakes continue to work properly when the wheel is bent.

Turn the bike upside down. If it's the back wheel, get behind the bike; if it's the front, get in front so that you're in line with the wheel. Spin the wheel and look at the area where it passes between the brake blocks (or, if you have disc brakes, where brake blocks would be). If the wheel is too wobbly to pass between the brake blocks, release your brake units. If it's too wobbly to pass between the frame, pick your bike up and start walking home.

If you think you can straighten the wheel, spin it a couple more times and look at its shape. You need to identify the point where the wheel is most bent – the biggest bulge away from the centre line. If you have V-brakes, use one of the brake blocks as a guide. Hold the brake unit still and spin the wheel, watching how the gap between the brake block and the rim changes. If the wheel is badly buckled you're going to have to make a rough judgment about where the centre of the wheel is, and work towards that. You won't get perfection in the field – just get it round enough to roll.

Adjustments of a quarter- or half-turn of the nipple are plenty. It's easy to start with a buckled but salvageable wheel and end up with a useless pretzel by going too fast. Much better to stick to small steps. Check the previous page if you're not sure which way to turn the nipple.

STRAIGHTENING A WHEEL

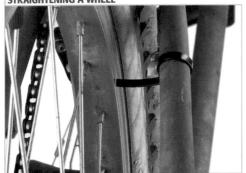

◀ **Step 1:** If you don't have V-brakes, you will have to improvise a gauge to measure the wobble of the wheel against. Zipties are invaluable here – either ziptie a stick to the chainstay or fork so that it sits level with the rim, or zip a tie around the fork or stay, leaving a long tag hanging off. Use the tag as your gauge.

◀ **Step 2:** Spin the wheel again and stop it when the middle of the biggest bulge is level with your gauge. Look at the spokes on the wheel. You'll see that alternate spokes lead to opposite sides of the wheel.

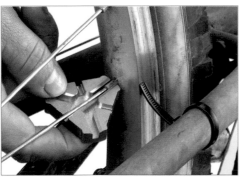

◀ **Step 3:** Choose the spoke at the centre of the bulge. If it leads to the same side of the wheel as the bulge, loosen this spoke and tighten the spokes on either side. A quarter- or half-turn should be enough. If the central spoke leads to the opposite side of the hub, tighten this spoke and loosen spokes on either side by a quarter- or half-turn. Spin the wheel again and pick out the biggest bulge.

Regular Checks

This section guides you through some basic routines that will make your bike safer, more comfortable and last longer. Check your bike is ready for you every time you go out for a ride. A quick, but thorough, safety check can prevent accidents, and help you to catch potential problems before you set out. Cheap, clean, lubricated components will work better and last longer than expensive ones that have been so neglected that they're dirty and crunchy – so if you want to save a bit of money, spend a bit of time on keeping your machine clean.

Cateye lights and computer

Twelve routine safety checks before you ride

Checking your bike every time you ride it can seem like a lot of effort and a little bit boring. It needn't take more than a few moments, however, and occasionally you'll appreciate the time it takes because you'll pick up a problem waiting to happen, which is far easier to fix before you set off. Looking carefully at your bike regularly also makes it easier to spot when something is wrong.

▶ Specialized Enduro Expert

It's worth having a routine for checking your bike. Doing it in the same order every time means you're less likely to miss something. It's worth going through a mental checklist at the same time to ensure you have everything else you need for a ride. Your needs will depend how far you intend to leave civilization behind, but normal items include plenty of water, emergency food, appropriate clothing, sunblock, map, tools and pump, as well as checking that somebody knows where you're going and when you are expected back. If you can rely on coverage, a mobile phone can be invaluable in an emergency. It's not a substitute for careful preparation though.

1) **Quick-release skewer:** Check both wheels are securely attached. Quick-release levers must be firmly folded to line up with the fork blade or rear stay; otherwise they can snag on things and open accidentally. Most levers have "open" and "closed" printed on opposite sides. Fold the lever so the "closed" side is visible.

2) **Tyres:** Check tyres for bald patches, tears and sharp things. The glass and thorns, etc., which cause punctures often take time to work through the tyre casing. Inspect your tyres frequently and pick out foreign objects. It's tedious but quicker than fixing the punctures they cause!

3) **Spokes:** Check for broken spokes. Gently brush a hand over both sides of both wheels, with the ends of your fingers brushing the spokes. Even one broken spoke weakens a wheel considerably. A permanent repair is also much easier if the wheel hasn't been ridden on.

4) **Front wheel:** Lift front end of the bike off the ground and spin the front wheel. Check it runs freely and doesn't wobble between the forks.

5) **Rim brakes:** Check the brake blocks don't touch the tyre or rim as the wheel turns. Rubbing blocks wear quickly and slow you down. Check position of the brake blocks. Each block should be parallel to the rim, low enough to avoid hitting the tyre but not so low that any part of the brake block hangs below the rim. (N.B. Photo opposite is of a disc-brake bike.)

6) **Disc brake calliper:** Check disc pads. You should have at least 0.5mm ($\frac{1}{50}$ inch) of pad thickness on either side of both brakes.

7) **Brake lever:** Carry out a simple brake check every time you ride. Stand beside the bike, push it gently forwards, then pull on the front brake. The front wheel should lock on and the back one lift off the ground. If not, don't ride!

8) **Brake lever:** Use a similar test for the back brake. Push the bike forwards, then pull on the back brake. The back wheel should lock and slide along the ground. If not, do not ride.

9) **Chain:** Check the drivetrain. The chain should be clean and should run smoothly through the gears without falling off either side of the sprocket or the chainset. Turn pedals backwards and watch the chain run through the derailleur. Stiff links flick the derailleur forward as they pass over the lower jockey wheel. It's worth sorting them out since they can cause your gears to slip under pressure.

10) **Cables and hoses:** Check all cables (brake and gear) for kinks in the outer casing or frays in the cable. Check hydraulic hoses for links or leaks.

11) **Stem:** Check that stem and bars are tight. Stand over the front wheel, gripping it between your knees. Try turning the bars.

12) **Pedals:** Check the cleats in the pedals. Make sure you can clip into and out of both sides of both pedals easily.

Regular cleaning routine

Cleaning your bike is the best time to spot worn or broken parts. Beware of jet washes though. Power hoses can leave your bike looking very shiny without much effort, but, no matter how careful you are, they force water in through the bearing seals, flushing grease out. This shortens the lifespan of bottom brackets, headsets, and other components radically. As a principle, start with the dirtiest bits and work up to the cleaner ones. That way you minimize the amount of recleaning you may have to do.

◆ Start with the drivetrain: the chain, sprockets, chainset and derailleurs. If the chain isn't too dirty, clean it with a rag. See chain hygiene on page 96.

◆ If your chain is too oily and dirty to respond to this treatment, give it a thorough clean. You can do a very respectable job without removing the chain from the bike, which is a lot of trouble and can weaken the link you remove. For the best results with the least fuss, tip a little degreaser into a small pot. Use a toothbrush or washing-up brush dipped in degreaser to scrub the chain clean. A chain-cleaning box (see page 16) is a good investment, making this job cleaner and quicker.

◆ Sprockets and chainsets need regular cleaning too. They're close to the ground and exposed to whatever's going around. If they're oily and dirty, it's worth degreasing them. Oil is sticky and picks up dirt as you ride along, wearing out the drivetrain. As above, use a little degreaser and work it into the sprockets and chainset with a brush. It's very important to rinse things very carefully afterwards to remove all traces of degreaser. Also, dry components carefully. Be careful not to get degreaser into bearings.

◆ Once everything is clean and dry, relubricate the chain. I prefer drip oils to spray types because you can direct the oil more precisely. Drip a little onto the top links of the bottom stretch of chain all the way around. Don't use excessive amounts of oil. Leave the oil to soak in for five minutes, then carefully remove excess with a clean rag. Don't worry about relubricating other drivetrain parts as they need no more than is deposited by the chain onto the sprockets.

◆ Next, clean the wheels. Muddy tyres are best cleaned by riding your bike along a tarmac road (with your mouth shut) once the mud is dry. Use a sponge and bucket of warm soapy water, hold the wheels upright to keep water out of the hubs, and sponge the hubs and spokes clean.

◆ Rim brakes work much better on clean rims. They pick up dirt from the ground and from the brake blocks, which stops the blocks from gripping the rim effectively, causing both rims and blocks to wear out prematurely. Green nylon Brillo pads are ideal for this job. Wire wool is too harsh but nylon gets detritus off the rims without damaging the braking surface. While you're there, check for bulges or cracks in the braking surface. These indicate that the rim is worn out and needs replacing urgently. If your rim has rim-wear indicators, check them now too.

● Disc rotors, the alternative braking surface, also work much better when clean. It's important not to contaminate them with oil. Use Finish Line disc cleaner for disc rotors. If they are oily, clean the rotors with isopropyl alcohol (from a chemist), which doesn't leave a residue. Don't be tempted by car disc cleaner – this leaves a residue that cannot be scrubbed off by the brakes.

● Brakes next. For rim brakes, release the V-brakes by pulling back the black rubber boot and pulling the curved metal noodle out of the hanger on the brake unit. Clean the block surfaces. Use a small screwdriver or knife (carefully) to pick out shards of metal. If the block surface has become shiny, use a strip of clean sandpaper to roughen it. When looking at the brake blocks check they aren't excessively or unevenly worn. Most blocks have a wear-line embossed onto the rubber. If the blocks originally had slots, make sure the slots are still visible. Once they disappear it's time for new brake blocks.

● For disc brakes, wipe the calliper clean. Check hydraulic hoses for oil leaks. There should be no trace of oil at any of the connections. Also check for kinks in the hoses. Look into the rotor slot on the calliper and check that the brake pad is at least 0.5mm ($\frac{1}{50}$ inch) thick.

● Clean and oil the parts of your cables normally trapped inside casing.

● For rear cable brakes, follow the black casing back from the brake lever to the frame. At the cable stop, pull the casing forwards to release it from the cable stop and wiggle the brake cable out of the slot. Use the same method to release the other sections of casing.

Run a clean rag over the part that's normally covered by outer casing. Relubricate each section with a drop of oil. Refit the outer casing.

● Repeat with the gear casing. You need to click your rear shifter as if changing into the highest gear, then push the derailleur away again (see page 116 if you are unsure how to do this). This creates enough slack in the cable to pull a section of casing out of its cable stop. Repeat with all the other sections of casing, cleaning and oiling – especially the last loop of rear derailleur cable. This loop is nearest to the ground and tends to collect dirt. Refit the outer casing.

● Pull the front derailleur out over the largest chainring, click the shifter as if to change into the smallest sprocket, then release the casing in the same way. Clean, oil and replace.

● Pedals are often forgotten, even though they get more than their fair share of mud and abuse. Use a small screwdriver to clear all the mud from around the release mechanism. Make sure you do both sides of both pedals. Mud gets forced into the springs every time you clip in with your shoes, building up until you can no longer clip in and out properly. Lubricate the moving parts sparingly with a light oil, like GT85 or WD40.

Clean the frame and forks. You need a sponge and a bucket of warm water to rinse everything off afterwards. All components work better and last longer if they're not covered in grime. Finally, a quick polish. Wax-based polish helps stop dirt sticking to the frame, keeping it cleaner for next time. Saddles also benefit from a polish – you might as well while you've got the polish out. Refit the wheels, reconnect the brakes. This is a good time to pump up the tyres, just to finish the job off neatly.

Brakes

Brake blocks and pads are very small – safe stopping depends on a contact patch the size of a couple of thumbprints per wheel. It's vital your brakes are adjusted to maximize this area. As you ride your bike you'll find yourself changing brake blocks almost as often as you have to fix punctures – so it's worth learning how to do it yourself.

This chapter also covers changing and adjusting brake cables, and bleeding hydraulic brakes. Properly adjusted brakes aren't just to slow you down – they actually help you go faster.

Disk brake rotors

V-brakes: a general introduction and how to manage wear and tear

V-brakes have now become standard issue on mountain bikes. They have superseded cantilever brakes and will in turn be made obsolete by disc brakes. However, they are cheap and simple to maintain, so we will start with them. Here follows an outline of the advantages and disadvantages of this braking system.

V-brakes overtook cantilevers in popularity because they are more powerful. However, there has always been a trade-off in terms of pad wear – cantilever pads last much longer. V-brakes stop you faster because the way they are designed pushes them onto the rim harder than cantilevers, wearing out both the rim and brake blocks faster. So enjoy the powerful braking, but remember that as a direct consequence you are going to have to learn to inspect brake blocks frequently for wear and replace them. Depending on where and how you ride you can wear out brake blocks at the rate of a set per day, and through a rim in a matter of months.

Regular maintenance
Keeping blocks and rims clean will make a huge difference to how long they both last. Dirty rims will wear out brake blocks, while flakes of grit and metal caught in your brake blocks will scour the rim surface. It's easy to forget that the rims are an integral part of the braking system. Unless they're clean and flat, the brake blocks will struggle to grip them and stop you in your tracks.

This section takes you through the processes of checking that your V-brakes are set up and working correctly, fitting new brake blocks and fitting a new cable. Careful brake-block alignment and smooth cables will help you get the most power out of your brakes.

You'll also get more feedback from them. Good set-up means that when your hands are on the brake levers you will be able to feel what effect the brakes are having, increasing your control over the bike.

Good brakes don't just lock the wheel up, they allow you to control your speed much more accurately.

One important thing to remember is that brake blocks and cables often just need cleaning rather than replacing. Cables can be cleaned rather than replaced as long as they're not frayed or kinked. Use the following procedure for replacing your cable. Keep to the instructions for removing the old cable, then clean it with a light oil like GT85. If necessary, soak congealed dirt off with degreaser.

Cut the end of the cable off cleanly so that it can be neatly threaded through the outer casing. Clean the inside of the outer casing by squirting spray oil through it to flush out dirt. Replace any sections that are cracked, squashed or kinked. Replace bent ferrules. Then refit as a new cable.

V-brakes: a quick checkup to help ensure performance every ride

However casual you are about bike maintenance, you need to make sure that your brakes are working properly every time you set off on a ride. This doesn't need to be a lengthy procedure – just give your bike a careful visual check before you head off.

The steps below make up a quick and regular check to keep your brakes in good running order and they give you warning when it's time for a more serious overhaul.

If the steps on page 58 indicate any problems, please refer to pages 61–64 and 67–69 for relevant repairs. Whatever you do, don't set off on a ride with brakes that don't work properly.

Lift each wheel and spin it to check the brakes don't rub on the rims or the tyre as the wheel turns. Look at the gap between the brake block and the rim on each side of each brake. See pages 59 and 61.

You'll need to disconnect the brake cable so that you can pull the brake blocks out from the rim. V-brakes are designed to make this easy. They also help when you want to remove and replace the wheels because you can get the tyre out past the brake blocks without letting the air out.

The brake cable

The brake cable arrives at the brake unit via a short curved metal tube called a "noodle" or "lead pipe" (pronounced as in "leading in the right direction", not lead, the heavy metal). The end of the lead pipe has a pointed head with a raised collar. The brake cable passes through the noodle and then clamps onto one of the brake units. The other brake unit has a hinged hanger with a key-shaped hole for the noodle.

The collar stops the noodle pulling through the hanger, so when you pull on the cable, the two brake units are drawn together, pulling the brake blocks onto the rim. The section of cable between the hanger and the cable clamp bolt is often concealed inside a black rubber boot that helps keep the cable clean.

To release the brake units, draw back the rubber boot to reveal the head of the noodle where it emerges from the hanger. Squeeze the two brake units together to create slack in the cable. Pull the noodle back and out of the key-shaped hole, then pull up to release the cable from the slot in the key-shaped hole. Let go of the brake units – they will spring right back from the rim.

To reconnect the brakes, squeeze the brake units firmly onto the rim. Pull back the rubber boot so that it's out of the way of the noodle and guide the head of the noodle into the hole in the hanger. Make sure it's seated securely: the raised collar must be butted firmly up against the hanger. Refit the rubber boot back over the head of the noodle. Pull the brake lever to confirm that everything is seated correctly.

CHECKING V-BRAKES

◀ **Step 1:** Inspect the condition of the pads. Release the brakes, pull each side away from the rim and check each braking surface is flat, has nothing stuck in it and isn't worn through. Reconnect the brakes, checking that the brake noodle is firmly and securely located in its hanger.

◀ **Step 2:** Squeeze the brake-levers and check that each block hits the rim flat, square and level. Brake blocks that are too high will cut through the tyre, causing explosive punctures. Blocks that are too low hang under the rim, wasting brake potential and creating a lip that eventually starts to snag on the rim.

◀ **Step 3:** Run your hand along each cable from lever to brake unit, checking for corrosion, kinks, fraying or damage to the casing – the brake cable pictured here needs replacing immediately. Pull the lever firmly towards the bars and check that each brake locks the wheel when the lever is halfway to the bars.

Brake blocks: keeping your eyes open for regular wear and tear

Inspect your brake blocks frequently for wear, replacing them as they get thin and pick up grit and metal bits. Worn blocks make for a useless braking surface and eat expensive rims for breakfast. Ignore this important task and your rims will wear right through the rubber of the block to the metal innards of the moulded pad. Brake blocks have a wear line indicating when they should be changed. If you can't see a wear line change the pads when they've worn to the bottom of the grooves moulded into the pad.

Even if you don't wear out blocks very quickly you should still change them periodically as they harden with time and don't work as well. Every year should do.

In between full changes, check on the condition of the pad and improve it. This is easiest to do with the wheels removed.

Release the brakes and remove the wheel. Look at the condition of the pad. It should be flat and even, without visible contamination. If you can see flecks of meta, use a sharp knife to pick them out carefully. If the pad had been sitting too low or at an angle it will wear unevenly, leaving a lip that gets caught under the rim and prevents the brakes from letting go properly. This is a waste of brake block and braking potential. Carefully cut the offending lip off with a sharp knife, then follow the instructions to reposition your brake block so that it contacts the rim more evenly. If the brake block sits too high, it will wear through the tyre – an expensive error.

Lightly sand the surface of the brake block with clean sandpaper. People often use a file for this, but shouldn't – it will hold metal

flakes from whatever it was you last filed, and flakes will embed themselves in the blocks. Clean your rims too. If they have sticky black streaks, use degreaser. Oil or tar on your rims will squeal alarmingly, allowing your wheels to slip through the blocks without slowing you down. A green nylon scouring pad works well for stubborn stains, and will scrub off contamination without damaging your rims.

Some brake blocks are designed with removable rubber blocks. The old, worn ones are removed by pulling out a retaining pin at the back of the metal cartridge and sliding the rubber part backwards. Replacement rubber blocks slide in in the same way and are held in place with the retaining pin.

Always make sure the open end of the cartridge faces towards the back of the bike, otherwise heavy braking will rip the rubber out of the cartridge. The replacement blocks can be stiff to slide into the slots in the cartridge; it often helps to dip them in warm water.

ADJUSTING BRAKE BLOCKS

◀ **Step 1:** Loosen the Allen key bolt on each brake block. Keeping the Allen key there, use your other hand to manoeuvre the block to approach the rim at 90°, not overlapping the edge, top or bottom. The front of the block should be 1mm ($\frac{1}{16}$ inch) nearer than the back. Tighten the Allen key firmly and twist the block to check it is secure. Push the unit on to the rim to check position.

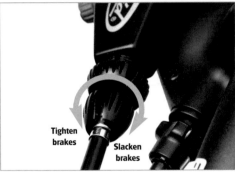

Tighten brakes

Slacken brakes

◀ **Step 2:** Spin the wheel; if the brakes rub on the rim, the cable is too tight. Undo the lockring on the barrel-adjuster at the lever. Loosen cable by turning adjuster clockwise. Turn twice, test again. When satisfied, retighten lockring. To loosen the cable further, return to brake unit, undo cable pinch bolt and release 3-4mm ($\frac{3}{16}$ inch) of cable. Retighten bolt and fine-tune adjuster.

◀ **Step 3:** Pull lever firmly towards the handlebars. The brakes should lock when the lever is halfway there. If it travels too far the cable is too loose. Leave enough space between lever and bar to hold the grips while braking. Undo lockring on lever barrel-adjuster and roll adjuster outwards. Test again and snug the lockring back to lever body.

Changing old brake blocks and adjusting their replacements

One of the points originally used to sell V-brakes was that changing the brake blocks would be easier than with cantilever brakes, which is certainly true, but can still be a bit fiddly.

The key is to set up the brake units so that they're parallel and vertical before fitting the brake blocks. Most new brake blocks come with a set of curved washers, but occasionally you'll have to reuse the old ones. Clean your rims at the same time for maximum grip.

CHANGING BRAKE BLOCKS

◀ **Step 1:** Undo and remove Allen key nut on the end of the old brake block stud, then wriggle out the old block and its curved washers. Now look at the position of the brake units. They should be parallel and vertical (A). Get the position of the units right before you fit new brake blocks. If they're not parallel, undo cable pinch bolt and pull in or release cable. Retighten the pinch bolts.

◀ **Step 2:** You may find the units are parallel but pointing off to one side. If so, use the balance screws at the bottom of each unit to even out the spring tension. This screw is normally a slot head but might be an Allen key. Choose the side that sits closer to the wheel and move screw half a turn clockwise. Pull and release the brake to settle the spring and repeat until brake arms are even.

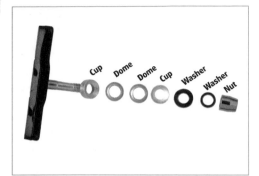

◄ Step 3: Check whether the brake blocks are designed for fitting in a particular direction. Any arrows should point forwards and the shape of the block should follow the curve of the rim. Each block comes with a collection of curved washers to space and angle the block. Their order of use varies from bike to bike and depends on the distance between the brake unit and the rim.

◄ Step 4: There should be a domed washer on the inside of the brake unit with the flat side facing the brake unit, and a cup washer between the dome and the brake block. Choose either the thick one or the thin one so that the block sits close to the rim, but not touching. A gap of about 2-3mm (around $\frac{1}{8}$ inch) is ideal.

◄ Step 5: The adjustment does not need to be perfect at this stage, just approximate. With the stub of the brake block sticking out through the slot in the brake unit fit the other domed washer, flat side against the brake unit. Then fit the remaining cup washer, followed by any flat washers. Finally, loosely fit the Allen key nut.

◀ **Step 6:** You will find that with this arrangement you can alter the angle of the brake block and also slide it up and down in the slot in the brake unit. Set it so that when you pull on the brakes the block hits the rim with the fixing bolt at 90° to the surface of the rim. The block should be level and none of it should hang over the top or bottom of the rim.

◀ **Step 7:** "Toeing-in": the front of the block (B) should be 1mm (¹⁄₁₆ inch) closer to the rim than the back, facing the same direction as the bike. Toeing-in helps stop your brakes squealing. Position the block and tighten the fixing bolt firmly. Check you cannot twist the block; the bolt must be firmly secured! Fit the other block the same way.

◀ **Step 8:** You will probably have to adjust the tension in the cable again to get the correct gap between brake blocks and the rim. For big changes undo the cable pinch bolt again, pull though or let out cable and tighten the pinch bolt. For a more subtle change use the barrel-adjuster on the brake lever. (See page 60.)

Readjusting balance screws

Finally, you will probably need to readjust the balance screws. Turn the balance screw clockwise to pull that side brake block away from the rim, but remember that this also pulls in the opposing brake block towards the far side of the rim. Pull and release the brake levers frequently as you adjust the balance screw because they have to settle into place every time. For a more detailed explanation of how to adjust your balance screw, see page 65. Check every nut and bolt to make sure each one is tight. Pull on the brakes firmly, and check that the wheel locks up. Spin the wheel and watch the brake blocks – if the wheel isn't completely true, you might find that the tyre rubs on the brake block as the wheel spins. Readjust the brake block position if necessary.

Choosing new brake blocks

This V-brake block set-up, using a threaded stud with curved washers, is used almost universally, making V-brake blocks completely interchangeable between makes and models. This might seem unremarkable but the situation with disc brake pads is completely different. Every make and model requires a specific pad – and nothing else will do.

The interchangeability of V-brake blocks has helped to keep the price down, since each manufacturer knows you can go elsewhere for replacements. Good makes include Aztec, Fibrax and Shimano. Longer or fatter brake blocks won't give you more braking power but are more durable. Slots cut in the surface of the block can help channel water away, but they can also collect grit if not cleaned regularly. Ceramic-coated rims need matching ceramic-specific brake blocks, which are harder than standard ones. Normal ones will wear away very quickly, as will ordinary rims if you use them with ceramic blocks.

Possible causes if the brake blocks are rubbing

You may find that, even after careful adjustment, one block or the other continues to rub. The most common problem is a wobbly wheel – if the rim is out of true, it will change position relative to the brake blocks as it revolves. For small wobbles, it's ok to spin the wheel to estimate an average position, then adjust the brakes to that position.

For wobbles larger than 2mm (0.08 inch), the wheel will have to be trued before the brake blocks can be adjusted correctly.

Toolbox

Tools for adjusting balance screws
- Usually crosshead screwdriver, occasionally 2.5mm Allen key

Tools for fitting or servicing brake units
- 5mm Allen key for brake-fixing bolts
- Oil to lubricate pivots
- Wet-and-dry sandpaper to clean pivots and to roughen braking surface

The balance screw

Each V-brake unit has a balance screw. You'll find it at the bottom of the unit, usually a crosshead bolt but occasionally a small Allen key. The end of each bolt rests on the end of the brake-return spring, so that the spring is forced against the bolt when you squeeze the brake unit towards the rim.

Turning the balance screw alters the preload on the spring, pushing its starting point further around the unit for a stronger spring action and releasing it for a weaker spring action. The confusing part is remembering which way to turn the screws for the effect you need.

- Turning the balance screw clockwise (A) pushes it further into the unit, increasing the preload on the spring, making it springier and pulling the attached brake block away from the rim.
- Turning the balance screw counterclockwise (B) unscrews it from the unit, decreasing the preload, softening the spring and allowing the brake block to move nearer to the rim.

Since the two units are connected together by the cable across the top, adjusting one balance screw will affect both units: if one unit is pulled away from the rim, the other will be drawn towards it to compensate.

To adjust the balance screws, look first at each brake unit from face on – the front brake from directly in front of the bike, the rear brake from directly behind.

If the balance screws are badly adjusted the units will point off to one side, rather than being parallel and vertical. There will be an uneven distance between brake blocks and rim, perhaps with one closer than the other, or even with one brake block dragging on the rim. To correct the problem locate the balance screws. Start with the unit that's closer to the rim and wind the balance screw in (clockwise) a couple of turns. You'll need to squeeze and release the brake lever every time you make a balance-screw adjustment to resettle the position of the spring. Look again at the angle of the two units. You should find that the adjustment has both pulled the closer brake block away from the rim and pulled the other block closer.

One confusing thing about the balance screws is that turning the screw has a different effect at different points – sometimes a couple of turns seems to make no difference at all, sometimes a quarter-turn makes a radical change. You'll have to experiment, adjusting the balance screws a quarter-turn at a time to find the central position.

◀ **Balance screws**

Check rims regularly for wear and tear

It's easy to forget that the rims are just as much a part of the braking system as the brake blocks. Every time you brake you're forcing your brake blocks against your rims. Powerful, controllable braking depends upon the condition of both blocks and rims. Whenever you brake you wear both surfaces.

Rim design is subject to two competing demands. When you're trying to go faster, it helps to have rims that are as light as possible. Your wheels are spinning around as well as along, so saving weight on them makes the bike feel substantially faster than saving the same weight on a static part of your bike like the handlebars. Ideally, the rims should be as thin as possible so that they don't weigh much. Light wheels make it much easier for your bike to accelerate, as well as facilitating changes in direction when you're moving fast.

But when you're trying to slow down, you need the rim material to be thick because the action of braking wears it out – and you don't want the brake blocks to wear through the rim. The truth is that rim manufacturers make their rims light so you buy them, but they expect you to keep them clean, so they wear as slowly as possible and to inspect them regularly.

Rim sidewalls

Having a rim sidewall blow suddenly is very alarming. Because of the pressure inside the tyre, the sidewalls don't give way gracefully. Over time the sidewall gets thinner and thinner. One part of the sidewall gets too thin to hold in the tyre. Then you brake suddenly – the moment of reckoning! Once one section of the rim starts to give way it cannot support

the next section, so within a fraction of a second most of your sidewall is ripped off. This punctures your tube, the resulting mess usually jams on your brake and you fall off the bike.

Some newer rims come with indicator marks that show when the rim is worn out. The rim will have a small hole drilled from the inside but not all the way through. The position of the hole is marked by a sticker on the rim with an arrow pointing to where the hole will appear. As you wear away the sidewall, the bottom of the hole appears from the outside; you can see your tyre through it. Time to get a new rim!

If you don't have a wear-indicator check the condition of the sidewall by running your fingers over it. It should be flat and smooth, without deep scours and ridges. Check both sides because one sidewall may be far more worn than the other. Curvy, bulging or scarred rims are due for replacement. If they look suspect, ask your bike shop for an opinion. If you find any cracks in the sidewall when you inspect, stop riding immediately.

It's also worth checking the join where the two ends of the rim meet. Sometimes, the ends don't meet exactly, making a bump in the rim that knocks against the brake blocks. Also check for cracks around the spoke holes and the valve hole. These are less dangerous but still mean the rim should be replaced.

Maintaining your cables

You should check your cables regularly for corrosion, kinks and damage to the outer casing. Over time, dirt and water creep into the cables. It happens slowly so you hardly notice the brakes are getting harder to pull on and are not releasing properly. Fitting new cables is easy. You will feel the difference instantly.

Cables generally come in either standard or fancy versions. The luxury versions tend to be either lined or protected by a sheath that runs from shifter to brake. Luxury cables can make a significant difference if you ride in very muddy environments, as they stop grit from creeping into the gap between cable and outer casing. However, they are generally much more expensive. All cables come with comprehensive instructions though, so we'll stick to standard cables here. You can either buy brake-cable sets in a pack with cable, outer casing and ferrules – Shimano make a good value pack – or you can buy the parts separately. Either way, you'll need a decent pair of cable-cutters to cut the casing to length; every bike has a different configuration of top tube lengths and cable-stop positions so the casing needs to be cut

for each one. The key thing to remember when cutting casing is to make a square cut across the tube so that the end of the casing sits firmly inside the ferrule. Look into the end of the cut casing and make sure there isn't a stray spur of metal across the hole. This will catch on the cable every time you pull and release the brakes, making your brakes feel sluggish. Use the sharp point of a knife to open out the end of the white lining that runs through the casing as it gets squashed shut as you cut the casing.

Fitting new brake cable
Before you start taking things apart, have a good look at how the cable is currently set up because you need to recreate that later with the new cable. Snip the cable end off the old cable and undo the cable pinch bolt.

FITTING BRAKE CABLE

◀ **Step 1:** Unthread the old cable from the brake noodle and all the way through the outer casing, leaving the casing in place. Turn the lockring on the barrel-adjuster and then the barrel-adjuster itself, so that the slots on both the barrel and the lockring line up with the slot on the body of the brake lever. Then pull the cable gently outwards, or down, to release it.

◀ **Step 2:** The nest, where the cable nipple sits, normally has a key-shaped hole so the nipple cannot pop out when you're braking. The most common fitting has a pivoted nest riveted to the lever blade with a slot in either the front or the underside of the lever. Wiggle the cable so the nipple lines up with part of the hole that it can pass through, and pop it out.

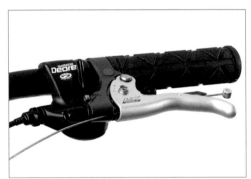

◀ **Step 3:** Some Shimano levers use a variation where the nipple is trapped behind a lip halfway along the lever blade. Once again, line up the slots on the lockring and barrel-adjuster with the slot on the body of the cable. You will need to flick open the plastic cover on the back of the lever blade, then push the cable towards the outer end of the lever. Wriggle the cable out from behind the lip.

◀ **Step 4:** Once you've removed the old cable from the lever, replace it with the nipple from the new cable, then slip the cable back through the slots in the brake lever. Feed the cable back though the sections of outer casing with a drop of oil. Feed the cable through the V-brake noodle, and sit the noodle back into its key-shaped hole in the hanger. Make sure it's lodged securely.

◀ **Step 5:** The cable normally clamps on above the bolt, but there will be a groove in the unit where you put the cable. Pull cable through, so there is a gap of 2-3mm (around $1/8$ inch) between brake blocks and rim. Steadying the cable with one hand, tighten the clamp bolt with the other. Leave about 5cm (2 inches) of exposed cable and crimp on a cable end behind the brake unit.

◀ **Step 6:** Test the brake; pull the lever hard twice. The cable might give slightly. Ideally, the brake should lock on when the lever is halfway to the handlebar. Use the barrel-adjuster to fine-tune; undo the lockring and turn it twice, away from the brake lever body. If the lever pulls too far turn the top of the adjuster towards the handlebars. Do a couple of turns and retest.

Replacing outer casing

If the new cable doesn't run smoothly through your outer casing it's worth replacing the casing – it could be dirty inside, or kinked. Replace one section at a time, so that you can use the old casing to measure new lengths. As you cut the casing, make sure the ends are neat and flat. Check that you haven't left a tang of metal across the cut end, and open out squashed lining with the point of a sharp knife. Each end of each section of casing will need a ferrule, apart from the last one that fits into the noodle – only fit one here if there's room for it.

Final adjustments

If you run out of adjustment on the barrel-adjuster (either it's adjusted so it jams on the brake lever body or it's at risk of falling off), go back to the cable clamp bolt, undo it, pull through or release a bit of cable, and retighten.

Then go back to the barrel-adjuster and make fine adjustments. Pull firmly on the brake lever again and check that it locks the wheel when it's halfway to the bar. Make sure that the brake blocks don't rub on the rims as the wheel turns. Check that every bolt is tight. You're done.

Disc brakes: one day all bicycles will be fitted with these

Along with suspension forks, disc brakes have been the major source of innovation in bicycles over the last few years. Once the preserve of only the priciest and flashiest machines they're now routinely specified on midrange bicycles.

There are two parts to a disc brake: the calliper, which bolts onto special mounts on your frame or fork, and the rotor (or disc), which bolts directly to your front or rear hub.

Disc brakes have two distinct advantages over rim brakes. First, they don't wear out your wheel by rubbing on the rim. Second, the hard surface of the disc rotor makes for powerful braking. Mechanical disc brakes are simpler to work on than hydraulic versions because they use standard brake levers and cables. Hydraulic disc brakes are more powerful but more expensive. Disc brakes of both types are getting lighter every year; new versions have barely any weight penalty over V-brakes. They still cost a fair chunk of extra money though.

Braking power

Braking power depends on rotor size. Large rotors, those with diameters of around 200mm (8 inches), are used for downhill racing where high-speed control is paramount. Cross-country racing, where maximum speeds are lower but weight is at a premium, tends to favour smaller rotors of 150–180mm (6–7 inch) diameter. As well as being heavier, larger discs are more prone to bending, which causes them to drag in the calliper slot.

Disc brake callipers are relatively simple to mount and need very little maintenance as long as they're kept clean. They're not in the direct firing line for anything that gets thrown up by your tyres in the same way that rim brakes are, so they will work better for longer in most conditions. People sometimes find them intimidating because they're relatively new and don't look much like anything else, but they're no more difficult to adjust than V-brakes. Bleeding is tricky, but none of the procedures are difficult. Brake fluid has to be treated with care: it will strip off your paintwork if you spill it on your frame, and stop your brakes from working if you spill it on the rotor or brake pads.

Precise adjustment takes a little care. In order to work effectively the calliper needs to be mounted so that there is a gap between the pads and the rotor on either side of the rotor. Since the rotor is bolted to the wheel, a location that cannot be changed, the gap is adjusted by moving the calliper so that it sits directly over the rotor.

Calliper adjustment

Calliper adjustment is the same whether the brake is mechanical or hydraulic. The calliper has to be bolted securely to the frame with a gap between the rotor and the pads on either side. Most hydraulic brakes work by pushing both pads onto the rim at the same time. These work best if there is an equal gap between pad and rotor on either side. Most mechanical disc brakes, and some hydraulic ones, work by pushing the outer pad onto the rotor, which flexes and gets pushed in turn onto the other pad so the rotor ends up being trapped between two pads. The system is more effective than it sounds! It works best if the gap between the rotor and the stationary pad is as small as possible to reduce the amount of flex in the rotor to a minimum.

Emerging standards

The concept of standardized component manufacture was invented for gun-making by Guillaume Deschamps for the French army. It encouraged the interchangeability between individual parts rather than the making of each gun as an individual mechanism. However, artisan gun-makers were so resistant to a process that damaged their trade that they prevented the idea

from realization for more than fifty years.

Bicycles are the same. Each manufacturer has its own way of doing things, and it takes a while for any one way to be universally accepted. A standard will emerge eventually, although it is not always the best of the options available.

The two styles of calliper fitting are the Post Mount, where the bolts secure the calliper point along the frame, and the International Standard mount, where the bolts point across the frame. Shimano took a few years to enter the disc brake market, waiting sensibly until everybody was sure it was a good idea. Their predominance in the market means that since they've chosen the International Standard it has become the norm.

▲ **Hope mini disc brake**

Disc brakes: naming of the parts

The rotor is the proper name for the disc that gives the disc brake its essential raison d'être. As with calliper fittings, it has taken time for the manufacturers to adopt a universal fitting. They seem to be settling on the "International Standard" 6-bolt fitting with a distance of 44mm between opposite holes, as originally used by Hayes.

The rotor can get very hot, particularly on long downhills. Don't touch it until it's had a chance to cool down or you really will burn yourself. It's also easy to trap your fingers in a spinning rotor while fiddling about with the callipers. Simply don't go near the rotors when the wheel is turning. Blood will contaminate the rotor surface as will the oil from your fingers, so avoid touching the rotor surface when adjusting brakes.

Each calliper is designed to take a specific size of rotor – the diameter and thickness are crucial. A larger rotor will give you more braking power and leverage, a smaller one will be lighter. Generally, a diameter of around 160mm (6¼ inches) is good for cross country; downhill needs around 200mm (8 inches).

Thinner rotors are used for single-piston callipers, where a moving piston forces the rotor across onto a stationary pad. Thinner rotors are more flexible. They take less force to bend sideways and snap back into shape as soon as you release the brakes.

Rotors wear out eventually, although it takes a long time. Shimano says its rotors can be worn down to 0.5mm ($\frac{1}{50}$ inch) thickness, but I would change them before this. For efficient braking, the surface of the rotor must be smooth and shiny. Torn or rough surfaces mean inconsistent braking and fast pad wear. Rough surfaces are often caused by the rotor rubbing on the inside of the calliper slot, so check the alignment carefully if you have to replace a rough rotor to make sure the new one doesn't go the same way.

It's vital that the rotor bolts are fitted securely; otherwise they will rattle loose. For this reason many manufacturers fit their rotors with Torx head bolts, which are a bit like Allen keys, but have star-shaped heads instead of hexagonal ones. The Torx type is no stronger than the standard type, but the unusual tool thwarts casual tinkerers.

Newer multi-tools, like the Specialized EMT tool, come with a Torx key; otherwise they're available from car and hardware shops. Don't try to tighten the bolts with a screwdriver or Allen key because you'll just damage the bolt head.

If you ride in muddy conditions you may find that a wavy-edged rotor, like the Hope Mini, will stop the calliper from clogging. (Those people at Hope on the northern English moors have plenty of mud experience.) Having your name laser-cut in the rotor gives little mud-clearing advantage, but it does let you identify your wheels amid a pile of dismembered bike parts in the car park.

Braking efficiency

Your rotors are your braking surface – your braking efficiency will depend as much on the condition of the rotors as on the condition of your brake pads.

Cleaning discs and replacing pads should be your first priority if you're not getting enough braking power. The majority of braking problems with discs are due to dirty or oily discs or contaminated pads, rather than more glamorous bleeding issues.

Cleaning rotors

Disc brake pads absorb grease or oil from any nearby source, with an immediate effect on braking power. Keep the rotor clean. It's best to avoid touching it with your fingers as they always leave greasy marks. Some people dab grease behind the brake pads to stop them vibrating and squealing. This is also a bad idea, since the grease will, without fail, work its way onto the surface of the pads. Clean the rotors with isopropyl alcohol, which doesn't leave a dirty residue. You can get it from a chemist. Car disc brake cleaning sprays are no good. Car disc brakes run much hotter, burning off the residue the sprays leave. Bicycle disc brakes don't get hot enough. Sometimes it can be worth cleaning new disc rotors straight out of the box to help reduce burn-in time. Bicycles that get a lot of city use need their rotors cleaned more frequently.

Replacing a rotor

Get the correct size tool; if you haven't got the correct one, drop the job until you do. If you round off the bolt head, it takes all sorts of messing about to recover. Undo each bolt a little bit, maybe a couple of turns. Once you can wiggle the disc on the hub, go back around again and completely remove each bolt.

The new disc needs to be fitted facing in the right direction. Usefully, some have a rotation arrow printed on the outside. Otherwise, if the rotor has an offset arm, the arm at the top needs to point forwards.

If you reuse the old bolts, put a strip of Loctite glue on each one. New bolts come pre-glued. Fit each bolt loosely through the rotor then into the hub. Take up the slack in each bolt so the head of the bolt touches the rotor. Check the rotor fits snugly against the hub. The order in which you tighten the bolts is important. Don't simply go round in a circle, alternate across the hub as shown below.

It is of utmost importance that these bolts are tight – loose ones will rattle out very quickly, which can be messy on the trail. Check they are still tight after your first ride, and then check again every 800 kilometers (500 miles).

▼ **Tighten rotor bolts alternately across the centre to hold tightening plates (A) in position**

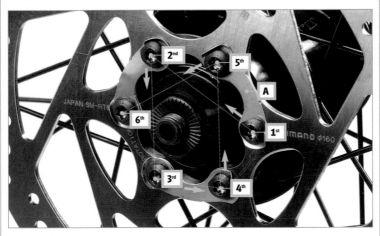

Mechanical disc brakes

These are often thought of as a halfway house between V-brakes and hydraulic discs. They're not as powerful as hydraulic discs, but they're cheaper. If you are intimidated by maintaining hydraulics the simplicity of cables is appealing. The advantages of not using the rim as the braking surface apply equally to mechanical and hydraulic disc brakes.

Mechanical disc units do tend to clog up quickly. Since they all work in slightly different ways there isn't room here to show how to service all of them, but they're very satisfying to work on. Keep the instruction manual and get into the habit of stripping them down, cleaning them and reassembling them. You'll be able to feel the difference right away.

The most common design consists of one moving pad and one stationary pad. The moving pad pushes against the rotor when you apply the brakes, bending the rotor slightly so that it in turn is pushed against the stationary pad and trapped between the two.

The moving pad is activated by pulling the brake cable. This pulls on the actuation lever on the brake unit, which twists the piston inside the unit. The piston is mounted on a shallow spiral, so that as it is turned it moves towards the rotor. Since the pad is mounted on the end of the piston it gets forced against the rotor. When you release the brake cable a spring inside the unit pulls the piston back from the rotor, ready for next time. Mud, dust and salt can work through the seals, getting trapped inside the mechanism. This makes the piston action sluggish, so it's well worth taking the time to learn how to strip them down.

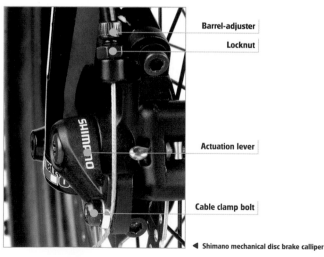

Barrel-adjuster

Locknut

Actuation lever

Cable clamp bolt

◀ Shimano mechanical disc brake calliper

Changing and adjusting cables

Mechanical disc cables seem to drag in less dirt than V-brake cables. The latter are affected by debris thrown up from the tyres in the same way – but corrosion and contamination in the cables still make your brakes feel sluggish. Fraying or kinked cables also need replacing.

Removing the old cable

Cut the cable end off the old cable. Undo the pinch bolt, then unthread the cable from inside the casing, leaving the casing in place. Work all the way back to the lever. They all work slightly differently, so you'll have to have a good look to work out how to extract the cable from the lever. Pull the lever back to the handlebar to make it easier to see inside. The most common arrangement is for the cable nipple to sit in a little pivoted nest inside the lever. The nest has a key-shaped slot, so that the cable can only be extracted while it's slack, preventing accidental release.

The barrel-adjuster and lockring will each have a slot along them. Line these up with the slot on the front or underside of the lever, and then wiggle the cable out and forwards or down. Now you can wiggle the cable nipple out of its nest. Watch how it comes out – you'll need to put the new one back.

Replacing outer casing

Remove each section of outer casing in turn, and cut a new section to the same length. Cut each end of each section squarely, making sure you don't leave a metal tang across the end. If the cable lining got squashed where you cut it, open it out carefully with the point of a knife. Fit a ferrule to each end of each section and refit the sections onto the bike. The exception here is the last section, which may not need a ferrule as it enters the brake calliper. Only fit one here if there's room. Make sure that the cable passes smoothly through each section of casing and that the sections are long enough for the bars to turn freely.

Fitting new cable

Now you're ready to fit a new cable. Reverse the procedure – again, you'll need to pull the lever back towards the bars to expose the nest. Check that the slots on the barrel-adjuster are lined up with the slots on the lever and slide the cable back in. Feed it through each section of casing with a drop of oil. Don't allow it to drag on the ground and pick up dirt. After the last section of outer casing feed the cable through the barrel-adjuster on the brake calliper and pull through by hand to take up any slack.

◀ Line up slots in barrel-adjuster and lockring, then pull cable forwards

CHANGING THE CABLE

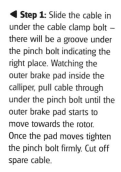

◀ **Step 1:** Slide the cable in under the cable clamp bolt – there will be a groove under the pinch bolt indicating the right place. Watching the outer brake pad inside the calliper, pull cable through under the pinch bolt until the outer brake pad starts to move towards the rotor. Once the pad moves tighten the pinch bolt firmly. Cut off spare cable.

◀ **Step 2:** The cable tension controls the position of the outer pad. Use the barrel-adjusters to set the cable tension so that the pad sits as close as possible to the rotor without touching it. Spin the wheel slowly while checking the gap between the outer pad and rotor. If you run out of barrel adjustment you may need to undo the pinch bolt, pull more cable through, and retighten firmly.

◀ **Step 3:** The stationary pad (on the inside, nearest the wheel) is usually adjustable. Use a 5mm Allen key to set its position so that it sits as close to the rotor as possible, without rubbing. Test the brakes – the wheel should spin freely, without rubbing, but lock on when you pull the lever halfway to the handlebars. If necessary, readjust the pad positions.

Mechanical disc brakes: adjusting brake pads for controlled stopping

The pad position will need adjusting after changing a brake cable, after fitting new pads or as the pads become worn. Ideally, the pad position should be set so that you can lock up the wheel by pulling the brake lever halfway to the handle bar. This gives you enough lever movement for precise speed control, without the risk of trapping fingers between lever and bar during emergency stops.

Mechanical disc brakes can be tricky to adjust. The clearance between pads and rim must be small without allowing the pads to rub on the rotor. A common source of confusion is that only the outer brake pad gets moved by the action of the cable, pushing the rotor against a stationary inner pad. This means that the two pads have to be adjusted in different ways.

You will really benefit from a workstand for this task. If that's not possible get a friend to lift the wheel off the ground at opportune moments.

Before you start adjusting, spin the wheel, look into the calliper slot and check how much clearance there is between rotor and pads. If the brake binds as you ride, one or both pads are rubbing on the rotor and need to be moved away. If you're finding that you can pull the rotor all the way back before the wheel locks, one or both of the pads needs to be moved towards the rotor.

The calliper slot is quite narrow and it can be tricky to see what's going on. Clean the calliper before you start trying to make adjustments. Then hold something white on the far side of the slot to make it easier to

see the gap. Spin the wheel while watching the slot. Unless they're brand new, rotors will often have a slight wobble. Make sure you adjust for an estimated central position.

Adjusting pad position

Before you start adjusting the pad position, ensure that the rotors are not dragging on the side of the rotor slot – this will damage the rotors and slow you down.

Adjust the calliper position (see the calliper fitting section, page 78), so that the rotor runs centrally before you adjust the pad position. Check that the wheel is properly and securely located in the dropout too – the rotor position will be affected if the wheel's not straight in the frame or forks.

It's worth keeping a spare set of brake pads. There is no standard size and shape (unlike V-brake blocks), so it can be tricky to find the right one.

Spares are light and easy to carry for emergency replacement, but it's far easier to adjust pads at home than out in the open because the job involves too many small fiddly parts aching to start a life of freedom in the long grass beside your favourite trail.

Mechanical disc brakes: adjusting Shimano callipers

The most common arrangement is that used by the Shimano callipers shown opposite. The position of the outer pad – furthest from the wheel – is controlled by the cable.

Tightening the brake cable moves the outer pad towards the rotor; loosening it allows the piston spring to pull the pad away. The inner pad, nearest the wheel, doesn't move when you pull the brake lever.

Instead, the outer pad gets pushed onto the rotor, which flexes towards the inner, stationary pad, trapping the rotor between the two. The position of the inner pad must be adjusted to be as close as possible to the rotor, without being allowed to rub.

Note that the rotor may not be completely flat. Little wiggles and bends don't matter, but you'll have to spin the wheel and watch the rotor to estimate a central position to adjust the pads to.

Alternative methods

Alternative arrangements for centring the pads over the calliper do exist, although the above method is now becoming standard since it's the easiest and most accurate way to set the clearance between pads and rotor.

Some older callipers have an integral adjuster, allowing you to wind the whole calliper sideways to adjust the gap between the pads. Turn the thumbscrew slowly. Once you get close, small adjustments make a big difference. Pull the brakes on hard between each adjustment to settle everything into place.

If the stationary pad is not adjustable, you will have to move the whole calliper sideways to set the gap between stationary pad and rotor. Then use the cable to adjust the clearance on the outside of the rotor. For Post Mount callipers, undo the two calliper mounting bolts a little – just enough so you can move them. Ease the calliper sideways, checking the gap beside the inside of the rotor nearest the wheel. This needs to be approximately 1mm (1/16 inch). Hold a piece of white card on the far side of the calliper to make it easier to see the gap. Retighten the bolts firmly. You may need to readjust the outer-pad spacing after this.

International Standard (IS) mounts are trickier. Estimate how much more gap you need for the pad to clear the rotor. Undo the calliper fixing bolts and add an equal number of shims between each bolt and the calliper. With normal washer-shaped shims, you need to remove the bolts completely. Shimano pitchfork-shaped shims can be slipped between the calliper and frame without removing the bolt.

Add shims until the inside pad clears the rotor, then retighten the calliper fixing bolts firmly. You may need to adjust the outer pad spacing again after this.

Wheel fitting

A surprisingly common cause of disc rub is a misaligned wheel. It's essential to ensure that the wheel is firmly and evenly fitted into the dropouts before you start adjusting pad clearance – a crooked disc will lead to a crooked pad adjustment. If you later refit the wheel correctly, the pads will rub. Dirt or paint flakes caught in the dropouts will prevent the axle seating correctly.

FITTING SHIMANO PADS

◀ **Step 1:** If the outer pad rubs, release tension in cable so the pad sits further from the rotor. Use the barrel-adjuster at the brake lever. Roll lockring away from body of the brake lever and turn barrel to roll the barrel-adjuster into the brake lever. Repeat until the brake doesn't rub, then wedge lockring back against the lever body.

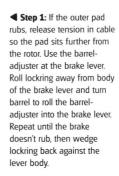

◀ **Step 2:** If you run out of adjustment at the barrel-adjuster make a coarse adjustment by undoing the cable-clamp bolt, letting out a little bit of cable, retightening the clamp bolt firmly, then repeating the fine adjustment (Step 1) with the barrel-adjuster.

◀ **Step 3:** If the inside pad is rubbing, you need to move the stationary pad away from the rotor. It usually requires a 5mm Allen key, which has to be threaded through the spokes of the wheel to get to the adjusting bolt. Normally, clockwise moves the pad closer, counterclockwise moves it away, but there are exceptions – watch the movement of the pad as you turn the adjuster.

Changing brake pads

Disc brake pads usually last much longer than V-brake pads. The material in the disc rotor is much harder than the material in the rim.

Make sure you get the right pad for the brake; the fittings and shapes vary between makes and even between models of the same make. Even if you know the make, the shape will vary from model to model and from year to year. After fitting, new pads need to be burnt in. Once you've got the new pads in, find somewhere you can ride safely. Ride along slowly, haul on the brakes and bring the bike to a halt. Repeat at increasing speeds until you're satisfied.

The pads on mechanical brakes sometimes wear unevenly. The most common design has the cable from the brake lever pull an actuation lever (mechanic's term for "lever that does something"), which pushes the outer brake pad onto the rotor. The rotor flexes under the pressure, gets pushed against the other disc pad, then ends up firmly trapped between two pads. This can cause uneven wear, but you must still change both pads at the same time even if one looks more worn than the other. They should be replaced

when either of the pads has less than 0.5mm (¹⁄₅₀ inch) of thickness left from any direction. You may need to take them out to check how they're surviving. If in doubt, follow the procedure for removing them below, and refit them if they have life left. Clean your rotors whenever you fit new pads.

Changing brake pads

Drop the wheel out of the frame. Look at the brake calliper. You'll see that it has a slot into which the rotor fits. Most often, the pads will pull out in the same direction that you pulled the rotor out of the slot – towards the centre of the wheel. Some will pull out of the top of the brake calliper, away from the centre of the wheel. Have a good look at the calliper before you start and draw a picture if necessary to help you put everything back together. There will be a pad on each side of the rotor and it will often have little ears or tabs to pull it out. Use these to manipulate the pads, rather than touching the pad surfaces.

CHANGING BRAKE PADS

◀ **Step 1:** Often the pads will not pull straight out; they will have some kind of device that stops them from getting rattled out as you ride. This will normally be a pin that goes through the opposite side of the pad, so look on the other side of the calliper for a retaining pin or split pin.

◀ **Step 2:** Pull out split pins, retaining pins or P-clips – keep them safe because you need to fit them back at the end. There may be one or two retaining pins. Split pins need to be bent gently straight with pliers before you can pull them out.

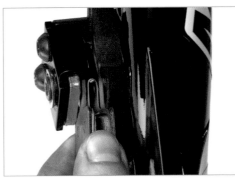

◀ **Step 3:** Gently pull the pads out, either by grabbing the little ears that poke out of the slot, or by pulling on the corners of the pads. If you're not sure of the correct replacement pads take the old ones to your bike shop to match them up.

◀ **Step 4:** The pads may have a retaining spring; make a note of its position and orientation and refit it with the new pads. Take care when fitting the new pads that the arms of the spring sit beside the pads, not over the braking surface. It's easiest to squash the spring between the pads, then fit both into the slot together, rather than trying to get the pads into the slot one at a time.

◄ Step 5: Slide the new pads back into the calliper, pushing them in until the holes in the pad line up with the retaining pin holes in the calliper. Refit the retaining pin or pins, bending over their ends, so that they don't rattle out. Then pull the pads firmly to make sure they are held securely in place.

◄ Step 6: Refit the wheel, wiggling the rotor back into the gap between pads. You may need to readjust the cable because new pads will be thicker than the old ones. Pick up the bike and spin the wheel. It should spin freely, without binding. However, it's fine if you can hear the pad rubbing slightly on the rim – this won't slow you down.

Brake-fitting tips

◆ Ensure you have the correct replacement pads, which vary between make, model and year of manufacture. Some packs come with a replacement pad spring, but, if not, you'll need to save the old one.

◆ Pads need replacing when they've worn down to 0.5mm (¹⁄₅₀ inch) thick.

◆ They will also need replacing if they've become contaminated with oil, which seeps into the brake pad material and prevents them from gripping your rotor.

◆ Some pad styles need a special metal spring that helps to force the pads apart when you release the brake lever. When fitting these take care to ensure that the spring sits beside each pad, not trapped over the braking surface.

◆ Avoid touching the surfaces of the pads, they will pick up contamination from your fingers.

Hydraulic disc brakes

Hydraulic brakes are much more powerful than cable-operated ones. The principle is simple: pulling the lever towards the bars pushes fluid down a narrow tube to the calliper, where the fluid pushes pistons outwards. The fluid is incompressible; any movement of the lever is transferred directly to the pistons. The pistons have brake pads on their ends, which are forced against a rotor attached to your wheel, stopping your bike on the spot. The whole idea of dealing with hydraulic fluid can be daunting, but as long as you're careful and calm, it's not difficult.

There are a couple of different fluid types. You MUST use the correct type for your brake. Using the wrong fluid ruins the seals in the system, causing leaks. The two basic types are DOT car brake fluid and mineral oil. Mineral oil is easier to work with because it doesn't damage paintwork and is less environmentally unfriendly. DOT fluid has a higher boiling point and expands less at high temperatures. There isn't a significant performance difference between the two types, just don't mix them up. Both types of fluid will eventually absorb water from the air and become less effective, so buy small containers and keep them sealed. Don't use half-empty containers of old fluid that have been sitting around, even if the cap has been on. I wear rubber gloves to work with both types of fluid, as it is worth avoiding skin contact. Brake fluid is very corrosive and needs to be treated with respect.

Sometimes air gets trapped in the system: For example, if you cut a hose to shorten it or you crash and tear a hose out. If this happens, the brakes feel spongy. Air is far more compressible than brake fluid, so when you pull the brake lever, all bubbles have to be squashed before the force reaches the pistons and starts moving them. Luckily, air is lighter than brake fluid, so if you open the

system at the top the bubbles rise up and out. The process of opening the brake, letting air out and replacing it with fluid is called bleeding. Bleeding is often treated as a complicated and mysterious process only to be carried out by druids. Actually, it's quite simple. Where people go wrong is treating bleeding as a universal cure for anything wrong with the brakes. It is only a useful method if you really do have air bubbles trapped in the system. It won't help, for example, if they have a leak somewhere or if dirt is hanging around your piston heads, making them sticky. If bleeding your brakes make no difference, it's time to consider whether the problem lies elsewhere.

You must also take careful steps to not get brake fluid or mineral oil on either the disc rotor or the brake blocks. If you are bleeding or filling brakes, remove the wheel, and remove the pads from the calliper to keep them safely out of the way. Do not refit them until the fluid is sealed back inside the system. If the system is open, and the pads are nearby, you will undoubtedly contaminate them. If this happens, replace the pads, and clean the rotors with isopropyl alcohol. It may sound as if I'm trying to make you buy more pads by saying contaminated ones don't work well, but they don't.

Adjusting hydraulic brakes

Every set of brakes works a little differently, making it impossible to give a comprehensive adjusting procedure without listing each individual type. Always keep the instruction book that came with your brakes and refer to it for detailed instructions for your particular brake.

It is fine for disc rotors to rub a little on the pads. The disc pads are much harder than rim brake pads, so a little bit of contact will not slow you down. Don't become obsessed by a little susurration when you pick up the wheel and spin it – you won't be able to hear it above the ground noise out on the trail. But a badly bent rotor – one that rubs on both pads as the wheel rotates – makes it really difficult to adjust the pad spacing satisfactorily.

Slight bends can be straightened by hand, but warped rotors must be replaced. The most common set-up for hydraulic brakes features pistons which will both push a pad against the rotor from the pressure of the hydraulic fluid on either side of the rotor. The more powerful variation is to have a pair of pistons on each side of the rotor, four pistons in total.

These are designed to fine-tune the action of the brake by making two of the four pistons slightly smaller. The smaller pistons will move first, followed by the larger ones. A single long brake pad fits over each pair of pistons. The extra length means more contact between pad and rotor, which also helps to keep everything cool. It also demands more precise calliper fitting because shorter pads are more forgiving of slight misalignments.

Adjusting pad clearance

The majority of hydraulic brakes are "open system", where the master cylinder on the handlebars contains a rubber diaphragm.

This flexes as the hydraulic fluid gets hot and expands, so that the pistons don't get forced on to the rotors by the extra fluid volume. Generally, these open-system brakes are adjusted by altering the lever position. Look for a small Allen key behind the lever blade, and set the lever position so that the pads bite when the lever is halfway to the bars. Note that this adjustment has no effect on the resting pad position – it just alters the clearance between the bars and the brake levers.

The less common "closed system" doesn't have the automatic adjustment of the flexible diaphragm and will have a volume-adjusting knob instead. With Hope brakes, it's a pretty silver wheel on the top of the lever. For Magura brakes, it's an easy-to-find red dial on the front of the lever.

◀ **Bleeding air bubbles from brake calliper**

Disc brakes: removing and changing brake pads

Brake pads must be changed if they're worn down to less than a third of their original thickness, so replace them if you only have 0.5–1mm ($\frac{1}{50}$ to $\frac{1}{16}$ inch) of pad left. You will also need to replace them if they become contaminated with oil. This could be the result of spilling brake fluid or of careless chain lubrication for the rear brake.

The way pads fit is similar enough with most models, which makes it possible for me to provide a general overview, but you should remember that each model has its own idiosyncrasies. It's worth having a good look at your calliper before you start taking out the old pads.

If you haven't got a photographic memory, draw a sketch to remind yourself how to put it all back together again.

All pads for all makes and all models are different, which is very irritating. You have to get exactly the right kind, so keep a spare set in case you need them when the shop's closed or it has run out of your type.

Removing the old pads

As a general rule the pads fit in position via the central slot in the calliper, either from the same direction as the rotor or from above the rotor.

You have to remove the wheel to get at them. The pads sit on pistons, which are inside the calliper. The pistons are pushed out when the brakes are activated, forcing the pads against the rotor and slowing the bike.

Pads have a flat metal base with the braking surface stuck on top.

Avoid touching the braking surface, as this will contaminate it. Use the metal base plate to manipulate the pads.

CHANGING BRAKE PADS

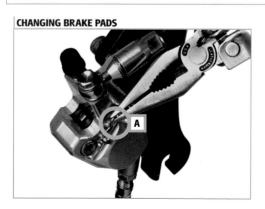

◀ **Step 1:** The pads might be held in place by a magnet, a spring clip on the back of the pads or an exact fit in the slot. There is often some kind of secondary security device to stop pads rattling free. Look for some kind of screwed- or slotted-in retaining pin, which goes through the calliper and through holes in the far side of the brake block, and remove them (A).

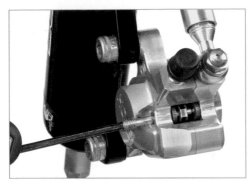

◀ **Step 2:** Extract the retaining pin. In this case, the pin is held in place with a 2mm Allen key. Undo the Allen key to release it from its threads, then pull out gently.

◀ **Step 3:** Pull the brake pads down out of the slots. Take care. Some have a spring that sits between the pads and holds them apart. Keep the spring as you need to reuse it; note its position. Have a good look at the pads as well – left and right may be different. Make a note so you can get the new ones back in the right way around.

Adjusting callipers

The new pads will be thicker than the old ones, so you have to push the pistons back into the calliper. If you have an adjuster on the lever which controls the piston position (for example, Hope Closed types), wind it out until the heads of the pistons are flush with the calliper body. For types without an adjuster at the lever, you will have to manually press the pistons back into the calliper. If the surface of the piston is flat a plastic tyre-lever is ideal. Push back the piston firmly so that it sits evenly in the calliper.

FITTING NEW PADS

FITTING NEW PADS

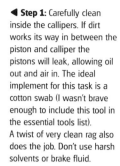

◀ **Step 1:** Carefully clean inside the callipers. If dirt works its way in between the piston and calliper the pistons will leak, allowing oil out and air in. The ideal implement for this task is a cotton swab (I wasn't brave enough to include this tool in the essential tools list). A twist of very clean rag also does the job. Don't use harsh solvents or brake fluid.

◀ **Step 2:** If there was a spring between the old pads, set it between the new ones, checking the orientation if left and right pads are different. Hold the pads and spring together, making sure the arms of the spring are beside, rather than on, the surface of the brake pad.

◀ **Step 3:** Slip the pads into the slot in the calliper. Push them home until the holes in the brake pad line up with retaining pin holes, refit retaining pins, and refit the spring or P-clips. Tug the pads downwards to check they are securely fitted. Refit the wheel. Check brakes. Pump the lever a few times to settle it into place – don't worry if it pulls all the way back to the bars the first time.

Bleeding hydraulic brakes

Bleeding isn't a regular task; as long as the system remains sealed, you can mostly ignore it. However, it does need to be done if there's been any break in the seal that might allow air in: for example, if you cut the hose to shorten it or you crash and pull out a hose. If you use your bike hard – for repeated downhill racing or for long downhill rides with the brakes working hard – the fluid will eventually become worn out from heating up too many times.

The procedure is the same regardless of the fluid, although DOT lasts longer – a year if you work it hard, four years with normal use. Mineral oil doesn't last so long, but it discolours when worn out, making it obvious when a change is needed. Pop the lid off the reservoir every six months or so, look at the fluid, and change it when it is cloudy.

Don't be drawn into thinking that bleeding has to be done routinely – you won't get an improvement in performance by bleeding unless something is actually wrong. If you have to bleed your brakes frequently there is something wrong. Look for leaks at all the joints and inspect the hoses carefully. The smallest split in a hose will let out oil and suck in air, making the brakes feel spongy.

Regardless of the specifics, the point of bleeding is the same: you are opening the system to release air bubbles, replacing the air with oil, then sealing the system again without letting in air. Here are the general guidelines, followed by specific examples.

Arm yourself appropriately. Most importantly, you need at least one, sometimes two, short plastic hoses to pump oil into the system at one end and to route surplus oil away from the bleed nipple at the

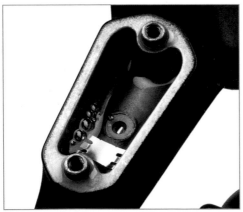

other end. With open-topped reservoirs, the surplus will spill over and you will need plenty of rags to mop up. Brake fluid is corrosive and will damage your paintwork if you let it spill onto frame or forks.

The easiest connectors come with Shimano and Hope types, which have a simple bleed nipple over which you can slip the end of the plastic tube. Other types of brake require a specific connector. You may have been supplied with the

◀ **Trapped air bubbles make your brakes feel spongy**

right connector when you bought the brakes or with the bike if the brakes were already fitted.

However, life sometimes isn't that simple, so prepare yourself for the bleeding operation by ordering the part from your bike shop. Plastic hose is easier to obtain because hardware stores stock it. Take the connection or your bike with you to ensure you get the right size. The larger, common size of bleed nipple – like that found on the Hope brakes – is the same size as standard car brake bleeding nipples, so you will be able to use bleed hose from auto parts stores.

Plastic syringes are very useful for pumping oil into the system. You can improvise by taping the plastic tubes onto squashable plastic bottles, but it's easy to slip and introduce air into the system, causing the bleed operation to fail.

Once the syringe is filled with oil hold it upright and tap the syringe to persuade air bubbles to drift upwards, just like in the movies. I often feel slightly foolish doing this, but it works. Once all the air has collected at the top of the syringe, squirt it out onto a clean rag so that the syringe contains only oil.

Surplus oil will be expelled from one of the tubes, so tape a bag or bottle to the end to catch it. Don't use thin plastic bags with DOT fluid – it's mildly alarming how quickly the brake fluid melts the bag. The tape is necessary to prevent it falling off as the weight of the oil increases, which can spread the stuff everywhere and spoil your bleed. All systems have a port at the lever end and a port at the calliper end.

Some systems, like Hayes, prefer to be filled through the calliper, with the surplus coming out at the lever end. Others, like Hope and Shimano, work best filled at the lever end with the surplus coming out through the bleed nipple at the calliper. Check your bike shop or your instruction book for the appropriate method for your particular brakes.

Bleeding Shimano Deore hydraulic brakes

The fluid used in Shimano hydraulic brakes is Shimano mineral oil. Don't use DOT brake fluid; it won't work and will eat the seals and leak. The oil comes in single-use packs, which contain enough fluid for one fill. Conveniently, this means that the container doesn't sit around absorbing water.

You'll be pouring fresh mineral oil into the reservoir, which can be messy.

Wrap cloth or kitchen towel around the lever before you start, as a preemptive mopping exercise.

The bleed nipple is narrower than the standard car size, so you'll need narrower plastic tube. You can find it in hardware stores, or buy a kit.

Clear plastic is best – you can see the oil and air bubbles emerging from the bleed nipple.

BLEEDING SHIMANO DEORE BRAKES

◀ **Step 1:** Start by removing the wheel and the pads of the brake you want to bleed to prevent them becoming contaminated by spillage. If you are bleeding the rear brake, remove the front wheel as well in case fluid spills out of the reservoir at the lever.

◀ **Step 2:** Loosen the brake lever fixing bolts and twist the lever, so that the top cover of the reservoir is level. Remove the top cover of the reservoir and the rubber diaphragm. Put these aside so that they stay clean.

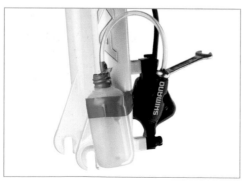

◀ **Step 3:** Shimano recommends you remove the calliper from the bike. However, bleeding seems to work if you keep the bike propped up so that the lever is higher than the calliper. Fit an 8mm ring spanner around the bleed nipple, and then push a piece of plastic hose over the nipple. Tape the other end into the mouth of a bottle and tape the bottle to your frame or fork.

◀ **Step 4:** Push the pistons gently back into the callipers, ideally using a tyre-lever. Wedge them in place with a block of clean cardboard. Using the spanner that you have already attached to it, open the bleed nipple a quarter-turn. Pump the brake lever gently, while keeping the reservoir topped up.

◀ **Step 5:** Flick the hose to encourage air to bubble up and escape through the open top of the reservoir. Shaking it sometimes helps too. Keep gently pumping the lever to help the bubbles rise. Keep adding oil and pump the lever gently until the lever goes stiff and only moves a quarter of its travel.

◀ **Step 6:** Pull the lever back, close the bleed nipple, release the lever. Fill the reservoir to the top with oil, replace rubber diaphragm and cap, catching the overspill. Gently tighten cap screws. Remove plastic tube from the bleed nipple and replace its cover. Refit pads and retaining devices, refit wheel and tighten brake lever. Pull and release the brake lever several times to settle everything into place.

Transmission

This chapter deals with the transmission – all the parts of your bike that transfer the pedalling power to your back wheel.

The parts that make up your transmission are relatively simple, but they are exposed to the elements all the time. They also have to be kept lubricated to work efficiently. If you don't clean your transmission regularly, oil and dirt will combine to form an abrasive grinding paste that quickly eats your transmission components. Since parts mesh with each other they often have to be replaced together, so leaving your bike dirty can be a rather expensive habit.

SRAM cassette

Transmission

Gearing up – or down – for the smoothest possible ride

If you only had one gear, you could set the bicycle up so you had to push very hard, but each pedal stroke would make the bicycle go a long way. This is a called a high gear. Alternatively, you could set it up so you didn't have to push the pedals hard, but one pedal stroke wouldn't take you far. This is called a low gear.

Both extremes work in their own way, but your body is most efficient pedalling at a medium rate – pushing moderately hard and pedalling moderately fast – between 80 and 100 revolutions per minute. Gears were invented so that you can maintain a steady pedalling rate ("cadence" – roughly speaking, how fast your legs are going round) while the bicycle travels at different speeds.

Mountain bikes are designed to have a very wide range of gears so you can maintain an efficient cadence both when moving very slowly – for example, up a steep, rough hill at 2 mph – as well as when moving very fast – for example, plummeting downhill at 40 mph.

Small steps between the gears allow you to make subtle changes from one gear to the next, matching your pedalling speed precisely to the terrain you're cycling over. In recent years, manufacturers have steadily increased the number of gears on your cassette, giving you smaller, subtler gaps between gears, making modern bikes more responsive than their old-fashioned counterparts.

Less haste, more speed

New cyclists – along with many who've been around long enough to know better – are seduced by the idea that in order to go faster, it's imperative to force the pedals around using as much strength as possible with every stroke. With experience, it becomes plain that this only gives an illusion of speed and, in fact, serves mainly to exhaust you in the short term and wear your knees out in the long term.

Generally, you'll get where you want to go faster, feeling less exhausted, by using a lower gear: your legs spin around faster, but you don't have to press down so hard on each pedal stroke.

◀ Shifting to a higher gear

How gears work

Gears are easier to use than before. Shifting was a complex art, inching the lever on your frame slowly around while listening out for the clatter of the chain. It protested at being dislodged from its sprocket, then the noise died down as it meshed. Now, chains slide noiselessly from one sprocket to the next at the the touch of a button.

What's great about modern cycling is that it allows you to keep pedalling at the same rate, regardless of terrain, by varying the amount of energy it needs to turn the back wheel. Ignore this page if you can't be bothered with the maths – it makes no difference to how much you enjoy your cycling.

Imagine you no longer have a spangly 27-speed bike. Instead, you have a bike with only two chainrings at the front, which you turn by pedalling, and two sprockets on the back, which push the back wheel around when they are turned. This leaves you with a 10-tooth and 20-tooth sprocket at the back, and a 20-tooth and a 40-tooth at the front. These combinations aren't useful for cycling, but they make the maths easier.

Start with your chain running between the 40 at the front and the 10 at the back. Start with one pedal crank pointing upwards, in line with the seat-tube. Turn the cranks round exactly once. Each link of the chain gets picked up in the valley between two teeth, so that, since there are 40 teeth on the chainring, exactly 40 links of chain get pulled from the back of the bike to the front.

At the back of the bike, exactly the reverse happens. Since each link of the chain picks up one sprocket valley, pulling 40 chain links through will pull 40 sprocket valleys around. But the sprocket you're using has only 10 teeth, so will get pulled round four times ($4 \times 10 = 40$). The sprocket is connected directly to the wheel, so in this instance turning the chainring one turn means that the

rear wheel will turn four complete turns. To measure how far this is, imagine cutting across an old tyre, to make a strip instead of a hoop, and laying it out along the ground. Measure the distance and that's how far the bike goes if you turn the wheel once. Turn the wheel four times and the bike goes four times as far.

For comparison, put the chain on the 20-tooth at the back and pop it on the 20 at the front. Now, turning the cranks around once only pulls 20 links of chain through, which in turn pulls the 20-tooth sprocket, and therefore the wheel, round exactly once. So, turning the pedals round once moves the bike forward one tyre length – a one-to-one ratio.

In the first example, the bike goes much further, but it is harder work to push the pedals around one turn. In the second example it is very easy to push the pedals round, but you don't go far. Sometimes you need to go as fast as possible, and you don't care how hard you work, so you use a combination of big chainring/small sprocket. Other times it takes all your energy simply to keep the wheels going round, so you need the easiest gear possible. Then you choose something like the last combination of small chainring/big sprocket.

Going back to the original bike you have seven, eight or nine sprockets at the back and three chainrings at the front. These allow subtle variations in how far, and easily, the bike goes when you turn the cranks. The aim is to maintain a constant cadence at a level that is most efficient for your body, over varying terrain.

Chain hygiene

A clean chain shifts neatly, whereas a dirty one shifts sluggishly and wears expensive chunks out of the drivetrain. To find out how clean your chain needs to be try reading the words stamped on the side plates. If they are legible, the chain is clean enough. If you can't read them, the chain needs your attention.

Ideally, clean your chain little and often – catching it frequently enough to only need a wipedown. This is both the laziest and the best method – take advantage of this rare combination! Leave your chain dirty for too long and you need to look at the deep-clean section later in this chapter.

After a ride lean your bike up against a wall and hold a clean, dry cloth or piece of kitchen towel around the bottom stretch of chain. Slowly pedal backward for 20 seconds, dragging the chain through the cloth. If it makes a big dirty streak, move to a clean bit of cloth and repeat. Job done. Simply do that every single time you ride and you maximize the chain's life without ever undertaking a boring major clean.

You need to lubricate the chain occasionally as well, but note that you can do as much damage by overlubricating as underlubricating. Chains need a little oil, but

no more than dressing for a salad. If the chain is squeaky, you've left it too long, and the chain is gasping for lubricant. As a rough guide, oil the chain every 160km (100 miles). If the chain collects greasy, black gunk as you ride, you are over-oiling.

As above, wipe the chain with a clean cloth. Drip a drop of oil carefully onto each roller on the top surface of the bottom stretch of chain. (Drip oil is much better than spray. It goes where you want with little waste.) The important thing is to allow five minutes for the oil to soak in (have a cup of coffee), then wipe off any excess with a clean rag – drag

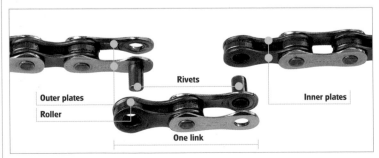

Rivets

Outer plates

Roller

Inner plates

One link

▲ Outer and inner plates, roller, rivets and link

the chain through it again. Oil is sticky. Leave it on the outside surface of the chain to pick up dirt and it makes a super grinding paste.

Cleaning your chain little and often like this ensures that it never builds up a thick layer of dirt, which means that you don't have to use harsh solvents on it.

This is well worthwhile – cleaning agents, degreasers and detergent will all soak into the internals of the chain, stripping out lubrication from the vital interface between the insides of the roller.

Each roller needs to be able to rotate freely on its rivet so that the roller can mesh neatly with the valleys between the teeth of sprockets and chainrings as you apply pressure.

Wax lubricants are an alternative to conventional oils. Several manufacturers make versions that work in similar ways. The wax sticks to your chain, protecting it from the elements but providing a layer of lubrication. The wax is not as sticky as oil, so it's less likely that dirt will adhere. But if it does, the surface of the wax will flake off, taking the dirt with it.

New layers of wax can be laid over the top since the surface should stay clean, saving you from having to clean the chain. This system means that your chain stays dry too, avoiding oily streaks on your clothes and in your home.

However, the system only really works if you start with a very clean chain – preferably a new one. A word of warning: never mix wax-based lubricants with normal ones – you end up with a sticky, slippery mess that adheres to everything except your chain.

▲ Laziest and best: a regular wipedown

Chain hygiene: deep clean

If your chain doesn't respond to the wipedown treatment, you must get serious. Dirty, oily chains need degreaser to clean them up.

This is strong stuff, so take care not to let it seep into bearings, where it breaks down the grease that keeps things well-lubricated. I prefer liquid degreaser, which you can apply with a brush, to the spray cans. Spray is more wasteful and harder to direct accurately.

Bike shops sell special sets of brushes, but my favourites are paint brushes. I cut off the bristles about halfway down, so what remains is firm but flexible. Keep the brushes you use for your drivetrain separate from those for frames, rims and disc rotors. Use rubber gloves to protect your hands from the degreaser.

Take your bike outside as this business always gets messy. Keep the bike upright, with the chain in the largest chainring at the front. Dip the brush into degreaser and work it into each link in the part of the chain that's wrapped around the front chainring. Do both sides, then turn the pedals around and work on the next section of chain. It takes a few minutes for the degreaser to work, so let it soak in, working around until you are back where you started.

Clean the chainrings next, front and back, picking out anything that's stuck between the chainrings or between the outer chainring and the crank arm. Clean up the derailleurs and the jockey wheels on the rear derailleur too, otherwise they dump dirt straight back onto the clean chain. Hold the back wheel upright and scrub the cassette clean. If there is compacted muck stuck between the sprockets scrape it out with a stick or skewer. Be especially careful with the degreaser at this point: keep the wheel upright to prevent it from getting into the rear hub or into the freehub.

Using a clean brush, rinse off all the degreaser with warm water. Jet-washing may be tempting but don't – ever! Dry the chain by running it through a clean rag and relubricate. Sprockets and chainrings don't need lubrication. Pop a drop of oil on the derailleur pivots, front and back.

Chain-cleaning box

A tidier option for regular cleaning is a chain-cleaning box. Fill the reservoir with degreaser, then snap the box over the lower section of chain. Pedal slowly backwards. Don't pedal too quickly or you'll splash degreaser out of the back of the box. Keep going slowly until you've used up all the degreaser. Unclip the box and take a five-minute break to give the degreaser time to break down the dirt. Rinse off with clean, warm water. Dry your chain with a clean rag and relubricate. It's worth cleaning the chain box for next time.

◀ **A chain-cleaning box helps keep everything tidy**

Measuring your chain for wear and tear

Your chain is under constant pressure as you pedal. A new chain arrives exactly the right size to mesh with the other components of your drivetrain.

Gradually, though, as time goes by and the miles rack up, the chain stretches. The gaps between each link grow and the chain inevitably elongates. Eventually, if you keep riding, the chain starts skipping over them instead of meshing with the teeth on the sprocket.

That's when you find yourself pushing hard on the pedals, expecting resistance. Instead of gripping, the chain slips and the pedal carrying all your weight gives way and spins like crazy, so you hurt yourself or even fall off. At this stage your chain is already worn enough to damage other components.

Joining the chain gang

If you are disciplined about measuring your chain carefully and regularly with a chain-measuring device, you can just replace the chain before it has a chance to wear the other components of your drivetrain.

This tool will tell you when you have reached this point. If you are attentive, you'll find it the cheapest option in the long term.

If you allow the chain to wear beyond this point, you will have to replace both the chain and the cassette at the same time. The old chain will have damaged the teeth on the cassette, so the new chain will be unable to mesh with it neatly.

The consequence of changing the chain without changing the sprockets is that the new chain will slip over the old sprockets, and, even if you can make it catch, the old sprockets will wear the new chain into an old chain very quickly.

If you allow the chain to wear so that it starts to slip over the cassette as you pedal, you will definitely have to change the cassette and probably some or all of the chainrings as well.

Look at the picture on this page and compare it with your chainrings – if they are starting to look like the example change them at the same time as the chain.

Note that you cannot compensate for chain stretch by taking links out of the chain to make it shorter.

The total length of the chain is not critical. It is the distance between each link that matters. If you take links out of a stretched chain, it is simply a shorter stretched chain.

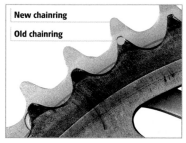

New chainring

Old chainring

▲ Worn teeth mean the chain slips over the chainring

MEASURING FOR WEAR

◄ **Step 1:** A chain-measuring device is the quickest and easiest way of accurately measuring your chain. The best are from Park Tools and come complete with an easy-to-read dial. Buy one today – it saves you time and money.

◄ **Step 2:** Alternatively, measure the length of 12 links. Twelve links of a new chain will measure exactly 12 inches (300mm). When it measures $12^1/_8$ inch or less, you can change the chain without changing the cassette. More than that, and you have to change the cassette as well.

◄ **Step 3:** Alternatively, put the chain on the biggest ring at the front and the smallest sprocket at the back. Hold the chain at three o'clock on the chainring and pull it outward. If the bottom jockey wheel of the rear derailleur moves, it's time for a new chain. If you can pull the chain off enough to see all or most of the tooth, you need a new cassette and probably new chainrings too.

Correct chain length and routing

It's critical to get your chain length right. If the chain is too long, it flaps about and the derailleur folds up on itself when it's in the smallest sprocket at the back and the small chainring at the front. Too short, and the chain jams when you shift into the big/big combination. These are not recommended gears, but everybody shifts into them sometimes. The right length of chain gives you the smoothest shifting and means your chain will last longer too.

The correct length chain is just long enough to wrap around the biggest sprocket at the back and the biggest chainring at the front, plus one link (a complete link is one narrow section and one wide section).

Fitting a new chain

To fit a new chain, first route it. Shift the two derailleurs so the rear one is under the biggest sprocket and the front one is over the biggest chainring. Start at the back at the lower jockey wheel and feed the end of the chain between the wheel and the lower tab. Next, feed the end between the top jockey wheel and the top tab. Route the chain around the front of

the top jockey wheel, then around the back of the cassette, forward to the chainset, through the front derailleur, around a chainring, and back to meet itself. Pull the chain as tight as it will go, as in the picture below – the rear derailleur will stretch forward to accommodate it. Add one link and calculate how many links you need to remove.

If you're rejoining the chain with a split link such as a Powerlink, remember to take this into account – you only need to add an extra half-link, because the Powerlink is half a link. Including the extra link, it means that, if you have to shorten the chain to remove a twisted link, you are still left with a working chain that can reach all the gears. Join or rejoin the chain and check through the gears. The chain should be long enough to reach around the big sprocket/big chainring combination with a little slack, but short enough so the rear derailleur doesn't fold up on itself in the small sprocket/small chainring combination. ▶

◀ Measuring the correct chain length

Correct chain length

To check whether the chain you have is the right length first make sure it's not too short. Step through the gears and check the chain will stretch all the way around the big sprocket at the back and the big chainring at the front. It's fine for the cage of the derailleur to be stretched forward in this gear, but make sure the chain isn't too tight – there should be enough slack to lift the middle of the lower section of chain up at least 2cm (roughly ¾ inch). Then, check it's not too long. Change gear into the smallest sprocket at the back and the smallest chainring at the front. Look at the rear derailleur cage – the lower jockey wheel will be folded right back, taking up the maximum amount of slack. Make sure it's not folded so far back that any part of the chain

touches any other part. The rear derailleur folds itself up to take up the extra slack created by shifting into the small sprockets and small chainring combination with the upper (guide) jockey wheel moving forward and the lower (tension) jockey wheel moving backward and up. If the chain is too long the derailleur will fold itself up completely in the small/small combination. If the lower section of chain gets entangled with the upper jockey wheel and derailleur cage the chain will rip the rear derailleur off as you pedal. Similarly, if the chain is too short, shifting into the larger sprockets at the back while the chain is in the largest chainring will stretch the tension jockey wheel forward. If there's not enough slack, the tension in the chain can cause the back wheel to jam or it can tear off the derailleur hanger.

Why chains break and what to do about it when they do

Some people never break chains, while others seem to break them every time they ride. Chains break for different reasons, including bad luck, but sometimes these problems can be avoided.

Sometimes small rocks or pebbles are kicked up by the tyres where they get trapped between chain and cassette. As you pedal, the chain breaks across the pebble. This is just bad luck and can happen to anyone.

Changing gears while stamping hard on the pedals puts a heavy strain on a few links. The links have to move sideways across your cassette to change gear, so they're at their most vulnerable because the pressure is applied at an angle. You do have to be turning the pedals to change gear, as this is what makes the chain derail, but your chain will shift across much quicker if you can

slacken off the pressure as you change. Even when going uphill try to anticipate gear changes, so that you can build up enough momentum to lift off the pressure momentarily. A well-adjusted derailleur will change from one sprocket to the next in a quarter of a revolution of the pedals, as long as it's not under too much pressure.

Your chain will be even more likely to break if the extra pressure from shifting coincides with a weak spot. Weak spots include anywhere the chain is twisted and anywhere the chain has been split and rejoined, so split your chain as little as possible.

Cassettes

Replace your chain every time you replace your cassette. Worn cassettes allow the chain to slip over the sprocket teeth, rather than to mesh securely into the valleys.

The standard fitting for attaching sprockets to the back wheel is the cassette. The cassette fits over the ratcheting mechanism, the freehub. This is bolted onto the hub with the bearing at the outboard end. The freehub allows the wheel to go round on its own without pushing the pedals, that is to freewheel.

The freehub makes a clicking noise when you freewheel. Cassettes and freehubs are made by different manufacturers, but all adhere to the standard Shimano-fitting pattern. The outer shell of the freehub is splined, a fancy way of saying it has grooves in it.

The cassette has a matching set of grooves to slide over the freehub. Everything is kept in place with a lockring that screws into the outer end of the freehub.

The first common cassettes were seven-speed. When eight-speeds were introduced, they needed a longer eight-speed freehub, but seven-speed cassettes and freehubs are not compatible with eight-speed ones. However, a nine-speed packs more sprockets into the same space, so nine-speed and eight-speed cassettes both fit onto the same freehub.

Removing the cassette

Remove the rear wheel, and take out the quick-release skewer. Note that, when you come to removing the lockring it makes a horrible noise when you loosen it. Don't worry! The lockring has a serrated surface that locks onto the serrated face of the cassette. These crunch when separated.

Lockrings that work loose can often be a source of lazy shifting – if the lockring isn't clamping the cassette securely onto the freehub body, the whole cassette will creep sideways along the freehub body when you try to change gear. This will also have the effect of causing the sprocket and freehub splines to wear prematurely.

REMOVING THE CASSETTE

◀ **Step 1:** Remove the quick-release skewer or nut, and fit the cassette-removing tool into the splines on the lockring. Make sure it fits snugly. Some tools have a hole through the middle so that you can refit the skewer or nut and hold everything in place, which is handy. Alternatively, for quick-release axles, use a tool with a central rod that slides into the axle and steadies the tool.

103

◀ **Step 2:** Fit a chain whip around one of the sprockets on the cassette in the direction seen in this picture. This will hold the cassette still while you undo the lockring. Fit a large adjustable spanner onto the tool – you need plenty of leverage so the handle will need to be about 30cm (12 inches) long. Choose the angle so that it sticks out in the opposite direction to the chain whip.

◀ **Step 3:** With the cassette facing away, hold the chain whip in your left hand and the adjustable spanner in your right. Push down firmly on both. If you bolted the cassette lockring tool on, loosen it once the tool starts to move, to make space into which the tool can undo. Remove the lockring, then slide the cassette off the freehub by pulling it straight out from the wheel.

Refitting the cassette

Wipe clean the splines of the freehub. Slide the new or cleaned cassette onto the freehub. Push the cassette all the way home. The outer rings are usually separate and must be correctly lined up. One of the separate rings may be narrower than the others and needs the supplied washer behind it. Grease the threads of the lockring, then screw it onto the center of the cassette. Refit the cassette-removing tool and the adjustable spanner, and tighten the lockring firmly. When the lockring is almost tight it makes an alarming crunching noise. This is normal!

◀ **Sprockets ahoy!**

Derailleurs

Derailleurs are cunning bits of gear. The way they work is simple: they take advantage of your pedalling action to move the chain smoothly from one sprocket to another. The name comes from the French for "derail" (pronounced simply "de-railer" or "de-rail-yer").

The rear derailleur hangs underneath the cassette and feeds the loose chain that's returning from the chainset back onto the cassette. This is the part of the chain that isn't under pressure – it's the top part that's doing the work as you pedal. The important part for changing gear is the guide jockey wheel, the one that sits closest to the cassette. It's also called the top jockey, even when the bicycle is upside down. The derailleur works by using the cable to move the guide jockey across the cassette. Because this part of the chain is not under pressure, the chain will follow the guide jockey and move onto a different size sprocket as it is fed onto the cassette.

The chain needs to be moving to mesh with a new sprocket, which is why you have to be pedalling to change gear. If you pedal too hard the chain will not be able to engage properly on the new sprocket, and will slip and crunch as you try to change gear.

The lower jockey wheel, also called the tension jockey, has a different function. It sits on the derailleur arm and is sprung so that it's always pushing backward. It is there because you need more chain to go around a combination of big chainring and big sprockets than for a combination of small chainring and small sprockets. The tension jockey is needed to take up the slack, otherwise the surplus chain would drag on the ground.

The derailleur is bolted on just below the rear axle. The top part stays still, but the knuckle, with the guide jockey attached, is hinged at an angle.

This means that as the guide jockey moves across, it also moves down, tracking the shape of the cassette. There is a spring across the hinge, pulling the two halves of the derailleur together. Consequently, left to its own devices, the spring will pull the derailleur so that the guide jockey runs under the smallest sprocket.

Finally, here's where you tell the derailleur what you want. The shifter on the handlebars connects to a cable, which pulls the two parts of the derailleur apart.

This moves the guide jockey across and down, and pulls the chain onto a larger sprocket. Moving the shifter the other way releases cable, allowing the spring to pull the guide jockey and chain onto a smaller sprocket.

◀ **Slave to the rhythm: the derailleur**

Indexing

In days gone by people used to be content just using the shifter to feel and listen for the right place under a particular sprocket when changing gear. Now indexed gears are universal. The shifter has notches instead of moving smoothly across its range and, if all the components are compatible and correctly adjusted, shifting one notch on the shifter pulls through enough cable to move the chain across exactly one sprocket on your cassette.

A few derailleurs are designed to work in reverse – the cable pulls the chain from the largest to the smallest sprockets and, when the cable tension is released, the spring in the rear derailleur can pull the cable back from the smallest to the largest sprocket. The Shimano Rapidrise (or Low Normal) derailleur is like this. Some people prefer it.

Adjusting your gears
Well-adjusted gears should be invisible – one click of the shifter and you should move into whatever gear you need without thinking about it. You need to lavish care on your

gears to keep everything running smoothly, though. Indeed, after keeping your chain clean, the next most important thing is to keep your gears well adjusted. They don't simply work better – your entire transmission lasts longer.

Get used to adjusting your gears before you tackle any other gear work, as you have to make adjustments at the end of many procedures, especially fitting new cables or derailleurs. The rear indexing is the most important adjustment – proper tuning is not difficult, but practice makes perfect.

The most important thing to bear in mind is that your gear adjustment depends on transferring an accurate signal from your shifters to your derailleurs, so that when you take up or release a length of cable at the shifter, exactly the same amount of cable is pulled through at the derailleur. This will not happen if the cable is dirty or frayed or the casing is kinked. If you find that the adjusting instructions aren't working for you, check that cable and casing are in good condition.

◀ **Teeth that bite gently: shifting sprockets**

Adjusting the rear derailleur

Adjusting your rear derailleur can be tricky. The same problem could have one or more different – but similar – causes. Your derailleur is going to need adjusting if it's slow to shift up or down, if it changes gear all of its own accord when you're innocently cycling along, or if it rattles and clatters whenever you change gear. This is how you do it.

Adjusting your indexing: Derailleur types – standard and rapid-rise

Before you start adjusting, use the following method to check whether you have a standard derailleur or a rapid-rise derailleur. Change into one of the middle cassette sprockets. Take hold of any exposed part of the derailleur cable where it passes along the top-tube or down-tube of your bike, and pull the cable gently away from the frame. Watch the derailleur:

◆ If it moves towards a lower gear (larger sprocket), you have a standard derailleur – follow the instructions below.

◆ If the derailleur moves towards a higher gear (smaller sprocket) when you pull the cable, you have a rapid-rise derailleur – adjustment is the same in principle as for standard derailleurs, but because the spring is reversed you have to start adjustment from the other end.

Shifter types – twistshifters and triggershifters

When you adjust gears you shift repeatedly through them to test what happens. All shifters work in the same way – adjusting your indexing will be the same process whether your handlebar gear levers are twistshifters or triggershifters. Start by experimenting to see what happens to the cable when you shift. Find an exposed part of the rear derailleur cable, like you did to check whether you had a standard or rapid-rise shifter, and pull the cable gently away from the frame with your left hand. Holding it away, use your right hand to change gear. You won't need to pedal at the same time, just operate the shifter. One movement makes the cable slacker, the other makes it tighter. Change up and down a few times so that you begin to remember which does what. For standard derailleurs, shifting so that the cable is tighter pulls the derailleur towards the wheel and onto a larger sprocket. Shifting to release the cable allows the derailleur spring to pull the derailleur away from the wheel towards a smaller sprocket. Once you are familiar with the action of your shifters, you can start indexing your gears.

People often get confused with gear indexing, mixing it up with adjusting the end-stop screw. This is also important, but it's different. The end-stop screws set the limit of the range of movement of the derailleur, stopping it from falling off either end of the sprocket. Sometimes they are set wrong and accidentally stop the chain from moving onto the sprockets at either end of the cassette.

If so, you cannot adjust your indexing properly – go to the section on end-stop screws on page 110, adjust them and then return here. Always check before you start adjusting the indexing that the chain reaches the smallest and largest sprockets, without dropping over the edge of either. To tune the indexing, pulling the cable moves the chain toward lower gears, the larger sprockets near the wheel. Releasing tension in the cable allows the derailleur spring to pull the chain outward, toward the small sprockets.

Adjusting the cable tension on standard rear derailleurs

This is possibly the single most important adjustment that you will learn to make on your bicycle and it's not difficult. There are always clear signs when you need to adjust the tension of your rear derailleur cable. If the derailleur doesn't respond to your shifter, if it shifts more than one sprocket when you click the lever, or if the chain rattles and clatters as you shift, it's time to look at your cable tension.

The important thing to remember during this procedure is to always start in the same place, with the cable tension at its slackest and the chain in the smallest sprocket. Otherwise it's easy to confuse yourself, matching up the third shifter click with the fourth sprocket, or whatever. You will either need a workstand, to keep the back wheel off the ground, or the assistance of a friend, to lift the bike up for you at the appropriate moment.

Before you begin changing the cable tension, familiarise yourself with the action of your shifter. Follow the casing that emerges from the right hand shifter to where it joins the top tube or down tube, emerging as bare cable. Hook your finger under the middle of this section of bare cable and operate your shifter – for trigger shifters, push and release one then the other. For twist shifters, rotate the shifter forwards then back. You'll feel the cable tension pull through, then release.

When the cable tension is exactly right, the chain sits exactly below each sprocket as you change gear. This maximizes chain life and stops the chain from clattering on the sprockets as you ride. Since the sprockets and shifter clicks are evenly spaced, once you have the adjustments for the two smallest sprockets the others should work automatically.

ADJUSTING REAR DERAILLEUR CABLE

You'll have to set up your bike so that you can pedal and change gear at the same time. This is one of those occasions when a workstand makes all the difference, lifting the bike off the ground so that the back wheel can turn and so that you can see everything that's going on.

The idea is to start with the chain in the smallest sprocket and the shifter in the slackest cable position, then check the gears by shifting across one sprocket at a time.

When the cable tension is exactly right, one click moves the chain one sprocket across. Increasing the tension helps the chain move to a larger sprocket; releasing tension helps it move back down to a smaller one. Big changes in cable tension must be produced by undoing the cable clamp bolt, pulling through or letting out slack and reclamping the cable. Fine-tuning – small changes in cable tension – are achieved by turning the barrel-adjuster.

Start with the shifter in high-gear position, and the chain in the smallest sprocket. Turn the pedals, and click once.

Ideally, the chain should move across to the next sprocket, and sit directly underneath it. Now move on to the steps outlined on page 109 opposite.

TAILORING THE TENSION

◀ **Step 1:** Use the barrel-adjuster to make fine adjustments. To get the barrel to move, hold it as shown with your thumb on the top of the barrel. Turning it one way tightens the cable and moves the chain away from you (A) onto larger sprockets. Turning the other way slackens the cable and allows the spring to pull the chain toward you (B) onto smaller sprockets.

◀ **Step 2:** If the derailleur doesn't move when you click the shifter the cable is far too slack. Undo the pinch bolt, pull through a little more cable by hand, tighten the pinch bolt. Start again in the smallest sprocket, clicking the shifter several times to make sure it is at the slackest position. Now increase the tension by half a turn and repeat until the chain lifts onto the second sprocket.

◀ **Step 3:** Once you can move the chain from the smallest to the second sprocket, try shifting back from the second to the smallest. You may find you have to tune the position further – try a quarter-turn at a time.

Adjusting the end-stop screw on your rear derailleur

The end-stop screws on your derailleur – also known as limit screws – prevent the derailleur from throwing the chain off either end of the cassette. This is a vital task: the end-stop prevents the chain from falling off both the largest sprocket into the gap between the cassette and the wheel and the smallest sprocket, so that it gets stuck between the cassette and the frame.

Either of these contingencies will damage your bike: cutting through the spokes where they join your rear hub or taking chunks out of your frame beside the cassette. The chain will get firmly wedged too, so the chances of you falling off and hurting yourself are quite high.

Only the heads of the end-stops screws are visible, the shafts of the screws are hidden inside the body of the derailleur. The derailleur is designed so that at either end, the tips of the end-stop screws come into contact with tabs moulded into the pivoting part of the derailleur. Screwing the end-stop screws further into the body of the derailleur means that the ends of the screws hit the tabs sooner, limiting the movement of the derailleur and preventing the derailleur from pushing the chain off either end of the cassette. If you set the end-stop screws too far in the derailleur won't be able to push the chain onto the largest or smallest sprockets.

It's easy to get confused when adjusting your rear derailleur because sometimes the same symptom can have more than one cause. For example, if you are having difficulty shifting onto the smallest sprocket, the cause could be that the "high" end-stop screw, which controls how far out the derailleur can move, is screwed too far into

the derailleur. However, too much tension in the rear derailleur cable can provoke the same response. For this reason, I find it easiest to adjust the end-stop screw when there is no tension in the rear derailleur cable. If you're fitting a new cable use these instructions to adjust the end-stop screws before you do so.

In cases where the cable is already fitted, release it from the cable stops on the frame so that it hangs loosely. To do this, first turn the pedals and change into the largest sprocket on your cassette. Stop pedalling and shift as if changing into the smallest sprocket. The chain won't be able to derail because you're not pedalling but the derailleur cable will become slack. Follow the outer casing back from the shifter to where the outer casing joins the frame at the first cable stop, and pull the casing forward toward the front of the bike. Wiggle the cable out of the slot in the cable guide. This will give you enough cable slack to adjust the end-stop screws without getting confused by cable tension issues.

Once you've finished adjusting the end-stop screws, replace the cable. To create enough slack in the cable, you'll need to push the rear derailleur toward the wheel so that it sits under the largest sprocket.

SETTING THE END-STOP SCREWS

◀ **Step 1:** Start by setting the high screw. Looking at the derailleur from behind, you see the two end-stop screws, marked "H" and "L", one above the other. Normally, the higher screw adjusts the high gear, and the lower screw the low gear. The writing is often small and difficult to make out. Turn the lower screw so that the chain hangs exactly under the smallest sprocket.

◀ **Step 2:** The low end-stop screw is trickier. With the back wheel off the ground turn the pedals with your right hand. Position your left hand with first finger hooked behind the cable entry tab at the back and thumb over the forward set of pivots. Push your thumb away from you (A) while turning the pedals. Push the derailleur across, so the chain runs to the largest sprocket.

◀ **Step 3:** If you can't move the derailleur across enough to shift easily into the largest sprocket, you need to unscrew (counterclockwise) the low "L" adjustment screw. Small adjustments make a big difference, so take it easy. If the chain threatens to fall too far, wind the low screw clockwise.

111

Rear hanger alignment

A lot is expected of your rear derailleur. You want it to be a precise, instant-shifting piece of gear even under pressure in a dirty environment. You need to be able to rely on it in all conditions and that's why it pays to nurture it.

One of the most common problems to be routinely ignored is the alignment of the rear derailleur hanger (the part on the frame that the derailleur bolts onto). The gears are designed to work when the two jockey wheels hang vertically underneath the sprockets. This vertical alignment is the first casualty of a crash, but it's often overlooked – you get up and brush yourself off, look at your bike and, if everything looks okay, you ride away. Bad things can happen next. If you've crashed and bent your derailleur inward, the gears may still work, but everything has shipped inboard a little.

Next time you stamp uphill in a low gear, you click the lever to find a bigger sprocket, but instead you dump the chain off the inside of the rear cassette, stuffing it into the back wheel just as you haul on the pedals. Likely results include falling off and hurting yourself – and expensive damage to your back wheel.

On a less drastic level, the shifting works best when the sprockets are aligned with the jockey wheels. The chain isn't being twisted as it runs off the sprocket; and the jockey wheels move in the direction they were designed to, rather than being forced up into the sprockets as they move across the cassette, which is what happens if the hanger is bent.

Look at the derailleur from behind. This way you get the clearest view of whether or not the chain is running in one of the middle gears. The sprocket, chain and jockey wheel should make a vertical line. The most common problem occurs when the hanger is bent so that the bottom jockey wheel hangs nearer the wheel, as in the picture below.

It's not unusual for the hanger or the derailleur to be twisted rather than (or as well as!) bent. Because this is a common problem all decent aluminum frames have a replaceable hanger.

There are many different types of hanger even within a make and model; the hanger you need might depend on the year the bike was made. To make sure you get the right one, take the old one to your local bike shop for comparison. They are almost never interchangeable.

If you don't have a replaceable hanger, the frame will have to be bent back. You can do it yourself if you are careful, but if you are unsure, this is a job I recommend you take to your bike shop.

◀ Hangers need to be flat and vertical to sprockets

Improving your shifting

It's often difficult to know where to start with gear adjustment. Sluggish shifting can result from a combination of factors, both constant and intermittent. The rear derailleur, in particular, relies on everything being set up perfectly so that all the components work together.

It's also tricky to adjust gears because they behave differently under pressure. Gears that feel perfect when you're trying them out in the garage can be disappointing when you try them out for real. Occasionally, the opposite situation occurs: you can't get the gears to shift properly at all in the shop, then you go for a ride anyway and unexpectedly they feel fine.

Adjust cable tension

If you're unhappy with the shifting the most sensible place to start is with the cable tension adjustment. Click the shifters all the way into their neutral position (high gears for standard derailleurs, low for rapid-rise) and then shift over into the neighbouring sprocket. If the chain doesn't sit vertically under the sprocket or doesn't shift crisply, you have an adjustment problem – see cable tension, page 108.

Check hanger alignment

Shift into the big sprocket and look at the chain from behind the bike. The chain should make a straight vertical line down the back of the sprocket and around the jockey wheels. If the jockey wheels are tucked in towards the back wheel, you have a hanger alignment problem – see page 112.

Replace or clean cables and casing

If your cable tension and alignment are correct, but your shifting is still sluggish, your gear cable may be dirty, kinked or corroded. In particular, check the section of outer casing that connects the rear derailleur to the frame, as it is vulnerable to getting squashed or kinked, and is near enough to the ground to pick up grit. For full suspension frames, the section of casing that links the front and back parts of the frame should also be replaced regularly.

Cables are among the least expensive parts of the bike, so changing them doesn't normally break the bank and will often make a substantial improvement to your shifting.

Clean or replace your rear derailleur

Your derailleur will work much better if it's clean and oiled. Give it a good scrub and oil it. Hold the bottom of the cage near the bottom jockey wheel and rock it gently toward and away from the wheel. Knocking, clicking or moving more than 4mm (around 1/8 inch) sideways indicates that the pivots in your derailleur are worn out.

Replace shifter

If none of these works, check that your shifter is sending crisp signals. Shift into a large sprocket, then click the shifter as if changing into a small sprocket, but without turning the pedals. This creates slack in the cable. Pull the section of casing that joins the bars to the frame forward and out of its cable stop. Slide the casing toward the back of the bike. This exposes the cable as it enters the shifter. Take hold of the cable and pull gently away from the shifter. Operate the shifter, checking that as you shift in either direction, the shifter pulls through little chunks of cable, and then releases them neatly, one at a time.

Front derailleur

The front derailleur lies directly in the firing line of all the dirt and mud that get thrown up off your back wheel, so it occasionally deserves a bit of care and attention. Cheaper front derailleurs don't last that long. I find they are the components least resistant to winter, especially if you ride on salted roads.

They get covered in whatever the roads throw up, accumulating mud that is then forced into the shifting mechanism every time you change gear. Eventually, the spring that returns the chain to the smaller chainrings can no longer cope and the derailleur stops returning when you release the cable.

▲ Front derailleurs are less complex than rear derailleurs

Front derailleur: adjusting the indexing

Like the rear derailleur, adjusting the indexing on the front derailleur is the same whatever type of handlebar shifter you have. Check what your particular shifter does by taking hold of an exposed section of cable and pulling it gently away from the frame.

Change gears in both directions to familiarize yourself with the effect that the shifters have on the cable. One of the directions or levers will loosen the cable, the other will tighten it.

Lift the back wheel off the ground for this procedure. Turn the pedals and move the front shifter so that the cable is in its slackest position. As you turn the pedals the chain should shift into the smallest chainring at the front. If it doesn't, the cable tension is too high. The barrel-adjuster for the front derailleur is up on the shifter. To loosen the cable, turn the barrel-adjuster so that the top of the barrel moves towards the front of the bike. Try a half-turn at a time to start with.

As with the rear derailleur, it is possible to get muddled between a problem with the cable tension or the end-stop screw adjustment. If you continue to adjust the cable tension, and the cable goes slack but the chain still doesn't drop into the smallest chainring when you change gear, you need to adjust the end-stop screws (A) – see pages 116–117. Adjust the end-stops, then come back here.

Once you've got the chain into the smallest ring, keep pedalling and change gear at the shifter by one complete click. The chain should climb up into the middle ring. If it doesn't, or does so sluggishly, you need to increase the tension in the cable – turn the barrel-adjuster so that the top of the barrel moves towards the back of the bike. Once the chain moves onto the middle ring, adjust the barrel until there is 1mm ($\frac{1}{16}$ inch) of clearance between the outer plate of the derailleur cage and the chain, with the chain in the smallest sprocket at the back. The chain should now shift precisely between the three rings. If it won't reach the outer or inner ring easily, you have to adjust the limit screws. They are especially likely to need adjustment if you have changed the position of the derailleur on the frame.

You may run out of barrel-adjuster – in which case you will need to turn it further out; but, as you turn, it drops out of the shifter, or you need to move it further in, but it jams against the shifter. If so, you need to make a coarse adjustment with the pinch bolt, then restart the fine adjustment. Roll the barrel most of the way back in, then undo the pinch bolt on the derailleur and pull a little cable through – start with about 3mm (around $\frac{1}{8}$ inch). Try the gears again.

Front derailleur adjustment is particularly sensitive to the position of the derailleur – if it's too high, too low or twisted, you won't be able to make it shift neatly by adjusting the cable tension. If you try the adjustment above and the derailleur still won't shift neatly, try adjusting the derailleur – follow the instructions for fitting a new one on pages 117–119. Similarly, a bent derailleur will not shift neatly. Once you've bent one, it is hard to persuade it back into the right shape. You are usually better off replacing it than trying to reshape it. It does work occasionally, but not very often.

▲ Derailleur position is vital for crisp shifting

Setting the end-stop screws

End-stop screws limit the movement of the derailleur so it cannot drop the chain off the outside or the inside of the chainset. If the chain won't travel far enough, even with correctly adjusted tension, check your end-stop screws.

Each end-stop screw controls the limit of the derailleur movement in only one direction. Identify the correct screw first – the marks are often printed in black on a black background. The inner screw usually adjusts the outer chain position.

SETTING END-STOP SCREWS

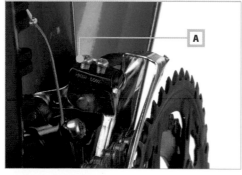

◀ **Step 1:** Start with the chain in the middle ring. Check the shifter is in the middle of the three positions. Turn the pedals and shift into high gear. The chain should lift onto the big chainring as you turn the pedals. If it won't go, you need to unwind the "high" (A) end-stop screw (marked "H" or with a wider line) on the derailleur. Unscrew the "H" screw a couple of turns and retest.

◀ **Step 2:** Once you've got the chain onto the big chainring, you need to make sure it won't go too far. With the chain still in the big chainring, gently roll in the "H" screw until you feel it touching the body of the derailleur – it will roll in fairly easily, then you will encounter resistance. At this point, back it off half a turn, and test again.

◀ **Step 3:** Try shifting into the smallest chainring. The chain should drop in first time. If not, back off the low adjusting screw (B). repeat until the chain drops neatly. If it drops in straight away, set the screw so the chain can't go too far. With the chain in the smallest sprocket, wind in the "L" screw, while watching the derailleur cage – stop when you see the screw start to make the cage move.

Choosing the right type of derailleur

You need to know three bits of information to replace your derailleur with the correct type – size, pull direction and swing style. There are only three frame diameters for the front derailleur to bolt onto – 28.6, 31.8 and 34.9mm (1⅛, 1¼ and 1⅜ inch). Shimano Deore front derailleurs get lots of fitting points, since they come in one size with the correct shims for the other sizes in the packet. You also need to know the cable pull direction. For top pull derailleurs, the cable

goes upwards from the derailleur, then along the top tube to your shifters. With down pull, the cable goes under the bottom bracket then up the top tube.

Check whether your derailleur is a "top swing" or a "conventional" one. Conventional types are the older design, where the cage sits lower than the frame clamp. Some full-suspension frame designs mean that this area is very crowded, so the "top swing" derailleur was introduced, taking up less space.

FITTING A FRONT DERAILLEUR

◀ **Step 1:** Shift into the little chainring to release the tension on the gear cable. Undo the cable clamp bolt, and release the cable from the derailleur. Next, undo and remove the bolt that fixes the derailleur to the frame. Fold out the hinge that clamps around your frame and pull the derailleur away from the frame.

◀ **Step 2:** The derailleur cage is still trapping the chain. Undo the small screw at the back of the derailleur cage. Ease the cage apart and slide the chain out. You will now be able to remove the old derailleur completely.

◀ **Step 3:** Undo the bolt on the back of the new derailleur cage, then slide the chain into the cage, bending it as little as possible. Support the back of the cage on the chainstay, so it doesn't get bent as you refit the cage bolt firmly.

◀ **Step 4:** Bolt the derailleur onto the frame. Start by positioning it at the same height as the old one. The correct height and angle have to be tested with the derailleur pulled out over the largest chainring. It's easiest if you test this by pulling it over by hand; things quickly get confusing if you connect the cable at this stage.

◀ **Step 5:** If it won't pull over far enough, undo the outer end-stop screw (marked with a wider line or an "H"). Pull out so that the outer cage plate is directly above the outer chainring. The front part of the cage plate should be exactly parallel to the chainring. If it isn't, loosen the fixing bolt, swing the derailleur around, and check again.

◀ **Step 6:** There should be a gap between the bottom of the outer derailleur plate and the top of the outer chainring of 1–3mm ($^1/_{16}$–$^1/_8$ inch). Test by pulling the derailleur out, then dropping it back and adjusting the height until it is right.

Adjusting a front derailleur

You'll need the back wheel up off the ground for this section. Turn the pedals and shift into the largest sprocket at the back.

At the front, with no cable tension, the chain should drop into the smallest chainring. If it doesn't, unwind the "L" end-stop screw. Then pull gently on the free end of the front derailleur cable and shift the shifter into the lowest gear.

Look carefully at the pinch bolt on the front derailleur and find the cable groove. Trap it in place and tighten the pinch bolt while keeping gentle pressure up on the cable.

Next, cable tension. Turn the pedals and shift into the middle gear. The chain should lift up onto the middle chainring. If it won't, or if the shift is sluggish, you need more cable tension.

Turn the barrel-adjuster on the shifter so that the top of the barrel moves backward, increasing the tension. Repeat until the chain shifts easily. Fine-tune by setting the tension, so that there is a 1mm gap between the chain and the outer plate of the front derailleur with the chain in the smallest sprocket at the back.

119

Fitting a new gear cable: triggershifters

Fitting a new gear cable is the easiest and cheapest way to upgrade your shifting. You'll need to arm yourself with a 5mm Allen key and a decent pair of cable cutters, as well as new cable, casing and ferrules for the ends of the sections of casing.

The procedure for changing cables is the same for front and rear shifters. Rear gear cables need changing more often because the section of cable near the back wheel gets filled with dust and mud easily, making your shifting sluggish.

For either derailleur, cut off the cable end and undo the cable clamp bolt at the derailleur. Pull the cable gently out of each section of outer casing in turn. Work all the way to the shifter, so that you end up with bare cable hanging out of the end of the shifter.

Follow the three steps on the next page to fit the new gear cable to the shifter, then route the new cable back through the outer casing to each derailleur. It's definitely worth changing the last section of outer casing on rear derailleurs every time, and any other sections that are kinked, splayed or dirty inside. If in doubt, change it! Cut each new section to length, using the old sections as a guide. Cutting the casing often squashes the lining inside – use a sharp knife to reopen the end of the lining. Fit ferrules to either end of every section of casing.

As you feed the cable through the casing, check that it slides freely. If the inner cable doesn't run smoothly through the casing now the gears won't work properly when you connect them. Replace any sections of casing that feel rough or sticky when you push cable through them. If you must use doughnuts (little protective rubber rings that stop the cable scratching the frame paint), use no more than two and make sure they're black. Feed the wire through the barrel-adjuster on the derailleur.

Check the action of the shifter by clicking through its range while pulling the cable gently away from the shifter – you should feel the shifter pulling cable through in steps. It should release in single jumps as you shift back. Replace any hatches that you removed from the shifter.

Paddle shifters

New XT and XTR shifters come as a combined unit with the downshift activated by the brake lever. The design is a cousin to the STI shifters that have become almost universal on road bikes. For cable fitting, follow the procedures for triggershifters, treating the brake lever as a gear shifter. To access the cable, remove the cover on these with a Phillips screwdriver. New cables should be lubricated as they're fitted. Any section that's going to end up inside outer casing needs a drip of oil. It doesn't need spreading about – it will gradually work its way around as you change gear. Grease is too sticky – it attracts dirt, which clogs up the outer casing. It used to be essential to put a dab of grease under the nipple as you fitted it. However, this is rarely necessary now – the nest where the nipple sits is invariably self-lubricating plastic.

FITTING A NEW GEAR CABLE

◀ **Step 1:** First pull gently on the exposed end of the cable, and shift into the gear where the cable is slackest. You may have to undo a hatch or remove a cover screw to expose the head of the cable – in this picture, a single crosshead screw is hidden between the triggers. A common variation is a pair of very small crosshead screws – take care, they will escape if you give them a chance.

◀ **Step 2:** Push the loose end of the cable gently into the shifter. If there are any slots on the barrel-adjuster, match them up with slots on the body of the shifter. As you push on the cable, the nipple will emerge from the hatch. You may need to twist it slightly to free it, or pull it free through the barrel-adjuster slots.

◀ **Step 3:** Without changing gears feed the new cable back though the shifter, reversing the procedure you used to get the old one out. Pull it firmly home so the nipple rests snugly in its nest in the shifter. Next, feed the cable through each section of outer casing in turn, with a drop of oil. Push the ferrule at the end of each section firmly into the cable stops on the frame. See page 108 to adjust cable tension.

Fitting a new gear cable: twistshifters

SRAM GripShift cables have an undeserved reputation for being difficult to fit. The very first models were a bit of a three-dimensional jigsaw puzzle, but current designs are much easier.

Precise shifting depends as much on your outer casing as inner – if the outer casing is frayed, kinked or jammed up with crud, it won't transmit a crisp signal between your shifter and your derailleur.

What you have to do is replace any sections that look unappealing as you go along. If you're cutting new sections, each one must be just long enough to reach, even when handlebars are in the turning position, but without excess. Each section must have a ferrule at either end, to prevent the ends splaying outward. You'll need a proper pair of heavy-duty cable cutters to chop outer casing – ordinary pliers won't do. Cutting the casing usually squashes the inner lining – open it back out with the point of a sharp knife before trying to push the new cable through.

You'll have to remove the old cable before you start. Cut off the cable end, undo the cable pinch bolt that clamps the cable onto the derailleur, and unthread each section of the cable back towards the shifter. Watch where it goes so that you can retrace each step with the new cable.

Cut off the old cable about 15cm (6 inches) before it enters the shifter. You'll need to shift into a particular gear to expose the head of the cable.

When you look at your gear indicators, one may be a different colour to the others or one of the numbers may have a circle drawn around it. If all the numbers look the same, shift into the highest number on the right-hand shifter (8 or 9) and into 1 on the left-hand side.

FITTING TWISTSHIFTER CABLE

◀ **Step 1:** Pull gently on the cable as it enters the shifter through the barrel-adjuster, and shift into the correct gear. Remove the escape hatch or slide it to one side, and look into the shifter. You may see the head of the nipple, or the head of a 2.5mm Allen key grub screw or a black plastic cover over half the nipple. If it's a grub screw, remove it completely.

◀ **Step 2:** If it's a plastic cover, pry it gently back with a small screwdriver. Push the exposed cable into the shifter. The nipple will emerge through the hatch. Pull the cable out of the shifter.

◀ **Step 3:** Without moving the shifter, slide the new inner cable in through the shifter. It will not feed in properly if the end of the cable is frayed, so cut off any untidiness. Pull it all the way through, make sure not to let the new cable dangle on the ground and pick up dirt. Replace the 2.5mm grub screw, if there was one, and tighten it firmly onto the nipple. Refit the escape hatch.

Other varieties of twistshifter

Some versions of twistshifters don't have a removable hatch – instead, the nipple is concealed under the edge of the rubber grip. Shift into the highest number on the right-hand shifter, or 1 on the left-hand shifter, and peel back the grip gently just below the row of numbers. You'll see the nipple – push the cable up through the barrel-adjuster; the nipple will emerge from the shifter. Feed the new cable back through without changing gear.

123

Triggershifters and Twistshifters: fitting cable to rear derailleurs

Fit the new cable into your shifters first, using the instructions on pages 120 and 122, then follow these steps to connect the cable to your rear derailleur. You'll need to adjust the cable tension once you've fitted the cables; see page 108.

Rear derailleur

For the rear derailleur, push the cable through the barrel-adjuster on the back of the derailleur. Lift the back wheel off the ground and turn the pedals so that the chain returns to its neutral position – the smallest sprocket for most derailleurs, the largest for rapid-rise types. Screw the barrel-adjuster all the way into the derailleur (turning it so the top of the barrel moves towards you), then back out a couple of complete turns.

Look carefully at the cable-pinch bolt; there are often several possible ways to fit the cable under it and only one of them makes your gears work properly. Look for a groove or a slot indicating the right place.

The most common place is on the far side of the pinch bolt, pointing almost straight forward. Once you have the cable in the right place, pull it gently to the right towards the front of the bike. Use the shifters to step all the way down and up through the gears. You should feel the cable pull your hand towards the derailleur as you shift down, then relax so your hand moves away as you shift up. Keeping a gentle pressure on the cable, change all the way up so that the cable is at its most relaxed and your hand is furthest from the derailleur. Guide the cable under the cable-clamp bolt and tighten up with a 9mm spanner or 5mm Allen key. Turn the pedals and shift all the way across the gears and back again. This will shake out any slack, so

undo the pinch bolt again, gently pull through any slack cable and tighten the pinch bolt firmly. Cut off excess cable and fit a cable end. Now you have to adjust the indexing; see page 107.

Rapid-rise rear derailleurs

Push the cable through the barrel-adjuster on the back of the rear derailleur. Lift the back wheel off the ground and turn the pedals so that the chain returns to its neutral position – the largest sprocket. Screw the barrel-adjuster all the way into the derailleur (turning it so that the top of the barrel moves towards you), then back out a couple of turns. Pass the cable under the clamp bolt – a groove in the derailleur will indicate the correct place. Use the shifters to step all the way down and up through the gears. You should feel the cable pull your hand towards the derailleur as you shift up, then relax so your hand moves away as you shift down.

Keeping a gentle pressure on the cable, change all the way down so that the cable is at its most relaxed and your hand is furthest from the derailleur. Guide the cable under the cable clamp bolt and tighten up (5mm Allen key). Turn the pedals and shift all the way across the gears and back again to the largest sprocket. This will shake out any slack in the cable, so undo the pinch bolt again, gently pull through any slack cable, and tighten the pinch bolt firmly. Cut off excess cable and fit a cable end.

Chainsuck: causes and remedies

You don't realize how annoying chainsuck is until your bike is infected. It can take patience to cure, as it may have several causes.

What is chainsuck?

Normally, as you pedal, you push down on the cranks and the teeth on the chainrings mesh with the links on the chain, dragging it forwards. The links on the chain also mesh with the teeth on the sprockets, dragging them around, which, in turn makes the wheel go around, propelling your bike, and making pedalling worthwhile. As each section of chain has been dragged around the chainring, it drops off the bottom and is pulled back along the bottom part of the loop, through the derailleur, and back up onto the sprockets.

Chainsuck happens when the chain fails to drop off the bottom of the chainset and, instead of heading backward toward the cassette, it stays stuck to the chainring, getting dragged up and around it as you pedal.

Cleaning and lubricating

First, try cleaning and relubricating your transmission, which is the cheapest option. If it makes things worse, you have at least one seriously worn component, which was just holding it together with its own layer of dirt.

Worn chain, chainring or both

When both the chain and chainring are new the distance between each link in the chain is the same as the distance between each tooth on the chainring. When you put pressure on the pedals, by dragging the chain around the chainring, the pressure is taken up by only the top few teeth.

The pressure then gradually reduces in each link as the teeth progress round the chainring, until at the bottom of the ring the links are released entirely and drop off freely, as intended. The pressure from the pedals is spread over all those teeth at the top of the chainring, reducing the amount which each chainring wears.

Once either chainring or chain is worn, nothing works so well. A worn chain on a fresh chainring engages only a single tooth at the top of the chainring, accelerating chainring wear. The chain links at the bottom of the chain get caught too far back in the valley of the bottom chainring tooth and are dragged upwards.

As the chain wears and stretches, the distance between each link expands. As the chainring wears, the valleys between the teeth get wider and deeper, allowing the chain to slip back in each valley under pressure.

Chain damage

There is only enough room between the sprockets for a straight chain link. A twisted one always catches on the neighbouring sprocket and causes the gears to slip or catch. A twisted link is also a weak point, so sort it out before it breaks and strands you in the middle of nowhere.

Chainring damage

Remove the chainset from the bike, and the rings from the chainset to get a good look at them. Check particularly for bent or damaged teeth. You can pick out the areas on each ring where the chain is having problems, as the adjacent chainring will be scarred. Twisted teeth are particularly irritating – they can be tricky to spot, but will hook onto the chain and lift it up and around, rather than releasing it at the bottom of the chainring. Bent teeth can be eased back straight with care. File off any tooth or part of tooth that protrudes sideways.

Wheels

This chapter leads you through the basics of wheel maintenance, starting with how to get your wheels on and off the bike easily when you need to and securely fixed to your bike the rest of the time. Your hubs will last longest if their cones are properly adjusted, as described on pages 130–131. If they're left too loose, your wheels will flop about as you try to steer you bike. Too tight and your wheels won't spin freely, slowing you down and wasting your energy. The last part of the chapter looks at your tyres, helping you choose some rubber that suits your needs.

Mavic Crossmax

The correct way to remove and refit wheels

Even if you do no maintenance on your wheels at all, it's important that you know how to take them off so that you can fix punctures. It's even more vital to be able to refit them securely – you really don't want to lose wheels as you ride along.

If you're not confident, ask your bike shop or an experienced rider to go through the procedure with you. When buying new wheels, if you're not familiar with the fitting system, ask your shop to show you how to remove and refit them.

The standard quick-release lever was designed for road-racing bicycles. It's a great system, allowing you to lock your wheels in place without tools. But the original designers of the quick-release lever had no idea what we would be doing with bicycles now. Suspension for bicycles existed already, but was a feature of butchers' and postmen's bikes and they seldom tended to use their machines for hurtling around off-road with six inches of suspension. The design has been modified along the way to make the fitting more secure – the "lawyer tabs" at the bottoms of your fork dropouts force you to undo your quick-release lever nut a few turns before you can release the wheel. This gives you a little more time to notice that something is wrong before your front wheel jumps out and plants you face first in the dirt. Similarly, the move from horizontal rear dropouts, which allow you to adjust the chain tension, was necessary to make wheels more secure. Once common on mountain bikes, these are now seen only on singlespeed-specific frames. The arrival of disc brakes has meant that hubs are subject to even stronger forces. Therefore, quick-release skewers need to be tightened securely and checked regularly. Forks for downhill and freeride often have chunkier release mechanisms, which aren't as instant, but are more resistant to accidental release. If you find that your skewers work loose during rides, take your bike to your shop for a second opinion.

There is some disagreement about the best position for the lever. Traditionally, quick-release skewers were oriented so that the lever was on the left-hand side of the bicycle and lay along one of the stays to prevent it getting caught.

On mountain bikes it's important that the levers don't point straight forwards, because they could get caught on a branch as you ride past and flip open. I prefer to fit them on the opposite side to disc rotors, as this reduces the chances of getting burned when fixing punctures. But the shape of your forks will often dictate where the skewer can fit, especially if there are adjusting knobs or fitting bolts behind the dropout. The most important thing is to ensure that the levers are firmly fitted. A ziptie around the skewer as an extra line of defence does no harm – I especially like Shimano XT skewers for this, as they already have a handy hole in them that's the perfect size.

FITTING QUICK-RELEASE LEVERS SECURELY

◀ **Step 1:** Your skewer and hub locknut should both have deep, sharp serrations for gripping the dropout. Always use good-quality steel skewers, which should make dents in the frame where they clamp the dropouts. There should be a small steel spring on each side – both of these should point in towards the hub.

◀ **Step 2:** Feed the skewer through the hub and screw the nut onto the other side. Hold the lever so that it sticks out at 90° to the wheel and tighten the nut finger-tight. Close the lever by folding it upwards, not by twisting it. You should feel resistance right away. The lever has to be loose enough to close by hand, but tight enough to leave a mark on your palm when you close it.

◀ **Step 3:** If it closes too easily, flip the lever open again, tighten the nut a quarter-turn and repeat. If you can't close the lever, flip it open again, loosen the nut a quarter-turn and repeat. If you haven't done this before, ask your bike shop to check that you have secured your wheels correctly before you ride your bike.

Checking and adjusting cones

Wheel bearings last longest when they are properly adjusted. The purpose of your hub bearings is to allow your wheel to spin freely as you pedal, while preventing the wheel moving from side to side in the frame.

The first part is obvious – hubs that bind instead of spinning will obviously slow you down and sap your energy. But play in your bearings will slow you down as well – if your wheel can move from side to side in the frame your braking surface (the brake rotor for disc brakes, or the rim for V-brakes) gets constantly dragged against the brake pads or blocks. Loose bearings will make themselves felt when you ride as well with wheels rocking within the frame, rather than tracking your movement neatly around tight twists and turns. Your bike will feel uncertain, with small unnerving pauses, before it follows your directions.

Checking for loose bearings is the same procedure for front and back wheels. Hold onto your rim, near where it passes between the forks or the frame. Pull the rim gently towards the frame. If the bearings are loose, the rim will rock towards you – you will feel, and maybe even hear, it shifting on its bearings. It's OK if the rim flexes a little, but it shouldn't knock at all. Loose bearings need to be adjusted right away – as well as affecting your ride they will wear quickly. If the bearings are allowed to bang onto the bearing surface, instead of rolling smoothly across it, they will create pits there. Check for tight bearings at the same time. Pick up each wheel in turn and spin it. The wheel should continue to rotate freely with just the gentlest encouragement. If it slows down prematurely, check the brakes first. If the brakes aren't the problem, your bearings are too tight. Use the steps on the next page to adjust them. Front-wheel bearings are easier to adjust than rear-wheel bearings because both sides are accessible. With rear wheels, the right-hand cone and locknut are buried under the cassette.

Adjusting your bearings

Remove the wheel from the frame and remove your skewer – it just gets in the way. Spin the end of the axle between your fingers, then rock it from side to side across the wheel. If you found your bearings were too tight when you checked the wheel in your frame, the axle will feel gritty now – it may not move at all. If it felt loose in the frame, you will feel a slight rocking as you move the axle from side to side across the wheel. Since the axle runs through the centre of the wheel, you only need to work on one side of the axle to adjust both sides of the bearing. The right-hand cones on the rear wheel are concealed by the cassette, forcing you to adjust from the left side. The front can be adjusted from either side, so just follow the instructions for adjusting the back axle.

Check that the right-hand locknut is locked securely onto the axle before you start. If this side shifts about as you work on the other side, you'll not be able to set the critical distance between the two sides accurately. Hold the short stub of threaded axle that protrudes out from the middle of the locknut and try to turn the locknut. If it moves easily with your fingers, you really need to service rather than adjust the hub. Dirt and water will have been drawn into the hub as the loose cones shifted on the axle.

ADJUSTING HUBS

◀ Step 1: Turn the wheel so that the left-hand side of the hub faces you. Remove any black rubber seals so that you can see the locknut nearest the end of the axle and the cone behind the locknut. There may be a washer, or washers, between the cone and locknut. Slide a thin cone spanner onto the cone and hold the cone still. Use a spanner to undo the locknut one turn counterclockwise.

◀ Step 2: The locknut and cone on the right-hand side of the hub are locked together, clamped firmly onto the axle, so you can hold the axle still by transferring your locknut spanner onto the right locknut. Leave the cone spanner on the left hand cone and turn to adjust the bearings – clockwise to tighten, counterclockwise to loosen.

◀ Step 3: Holding the cone still, transfer the spanner back to the left-hand side of the hub and tighten firmly onto the cone in its new position. Check the bearing adjustment again – it can take several attempts to get the cone position right. Refit seals, skewer and back wheel. Check the bearing adjustment once you've got the wheel back in the frame – you may need to readjust.

Tyres: which type suit you?

Everybody makes tyres. They all look different and everybody claims theirs are the best. I don't know how they can all be the best, but many people are more loyal to their favourite brand of tyre than to their favourite saddle manufacturer. Generally speaking, the tyre pattern is determined by the terrain you ride and the type of riding you do.

If conditions are very muddy, broad tyres – with widely spaced bars running across the rear tyre – grip where nothing else can. For harder terrain use something with closer lugs that has less rolling resistance. Heavier riders need a wider tyre; lighter people can get away with something narrower.

Because front tyres perform a different job to rear ones, their tread patterns are often different.

Front tyres are mainly concerned with steering so the lugs on the tyres are sometimes long bars pointing in the bike's direction of travel. This tread helps the front wheel grip as you turn corners, taking up the new direction and allowing the rest of the bike to follow.

Rear tyres are mainly concerned with propulsion (although they obviously have a part to play in how your bike corners), and so they often have wide bars across the tyre that grip the ground as you pedal. Different patterns work well in different terrains. Wide, deep paddles with big gaps are good for muddy conditions because they clear quickly. Closer, shorter lugs are better for harder terrain, rolling more smoothly so that you move faster.

However, your choice of tyre matters far less than its condition. When tyres are new the lugs have sharp edges and grip the ground securely.

Gradually the biting surface wears down, leaving the leading edge of each lug dull and chewed. Replace them and you ride more

confidently right away. Whatever the debate over this tyre pattern and that tyre pattern, a fresh tyre of any description always grips better than a worn tyre.

UST tubeless tyres

The UST (Universal Standard for Tubeless) tubeless tyre was developed to reduce weight at the wheel and to stop the tube getting pinched between the rim and sharp rocks, by doing away with the tube altogether.

The bead of the tyre and the inside of the rim wall are designed so that, when the tyre is inflated the two parts lock together, forming an airtight seal. Tyre and rim manufacturers agreed on a common standard, called UST, to ensure that everyone's tyres fit everyone else's rims.

The design is favoured by people who race because the weight-saving makes most difference to them. The tyres do lose air quicker than a standard tyre 'n' tube, so there's a balance to be considered. (Personally, I'd rather live with the extra weight than mess about pumping up my tyres daily, but I accepted long ago that there's no bike in the world light enough that someone as lazy as me is going to win a race on.)

If every gram counts or you like to run really low pressures for the extra grip, UST is worth it. If you like the convenience of jumping spontaneously on your bike without always pumping up the tyres, stick to normal tube 'n' tyre arrangements until they make USTs that don't leak.

Patching UST tubeless tyres

Although flats are less likely with UST tyres, they do still happen. If you're out riding, often the easiest thing to do is to stick an ordinary tube into the tyre and fix it when you get home. Once you get home, patch the tyre. Tyres are expensive and patches work, so it's worth the effort.

Finding the hole can be the tricky part! Pump as much air as you can into the tyre, and listen for hissing from the hole. Look carefully for a thorn or other spiky object sticking out of the carcass. Sometimes the hole is tiny and hard to locate and you have to submerge the inflated wheel in water to look for the bubbles. Once you've located the hole, mark it carefully or you will lose the place! Undo the thumbnut on the valve and let all the air out of the tyre.

It's important to do this next stage carefully. Both sides of the tyre have an airtight seal against the rim. It's much, much easier to refit the tyre if you only break one of the seals. If the hole is nearer one side of the tyre, start with that side. Push the sidewall of the tyre in and away from the rim. It will resist at first because the seal is tight.

If all else fails, lay the wheel on the ground and stand carefully on the sidewall of the tyre, as close to the rim as you can get. Don't stand on the rim – you'll bend it. Pull off the released side of the tyre all the way round and locate your hole from the inside. Pull out whatever it was that caused the puncture. Use clean sandpaper to roughen up the area of the tyre around the hole. If you're used to patching tubes, don't underestimate this part: you'll need to make this area bigger than the patch and much rougher than you would with a tube.

Spread the special UST glue round the hole. Make the area of glue much bigger than the size of the patch. Leave the glue to dry. Don't touch or poke it, just leave it. It needs 5–10 minutes – if it's cold, give it the full 10 minutes.

The next stage

You'll find that your patch is trapped between two layers of plastic or a layer of plastic and a layer of foil. Peel off one layer, but don't touch the surface of the patch with your fingers at all or it won't stick. Use the other layer of packaging to hold it. Lay it carefully onto the glue. With the packaging still on there, press the patch firmly onto the tyre. A tyre-lever is perfect for this as is the flat side of a spanner or a spoon.

You can peel the backing off the patch now, but I usually leave it there – it doesn't weigh much. Starting opposite the valve refit the tyre onto the rim. The tyres are unwieldy and it can feel like you need three hands, but once you've got most of the tyre on, it stays in place.

This last part is harder. Don't be tempted to use tyre-levers because if you do your tyre will leak forever. Fold the tyre onto the rim with your thumbs. Aim to finish at the valve. If it gets tough, return to the opposite side of the rim and massage the bead of the tyre into the well at the centre of the rim to gain enough slack to pop it on at the top. Once it's in, ensure that the bead of the tyre sits beside the valve, not on it, and pump it up. Be very vigorous at first to seal the tyre and keep pumping until it pops into place.

Big workshop track pumps are better at getting the initial volume of air in fast enough; very small mini-pumps can make hard work of this. Air canisters can be hit-and-miss. If the tyre seals right away, they're quick enough; if it doesn't, you waste the canister.

Try to take a spare inner tube with you out on your bike

It's always worth carrying a spare tube when you go out for a ride, because it's much easier to pop a spare tube in than to fix a puncture by the side of the trail. But it's definitely worth backing the spare up with a patch kit. Punctures often come in batches and carrying more than one spare tube gets bulky. So, hold onto your punctured tube and fix the puncture at your next opportunity. The repaired tube can become your new spare.

Fixing punctures

To repair a punctured tube, start by locating the hole. Pump up the tube to about twice the original diameter. You might be able to hear the air hissing out of the hole right away and locate the puncture that way. If not, lick the palm of your hand and move it along the tube, about half an inch away; you'll feel the cold air from the puncture on your hand. Roughen the area with the sandpaper from the patch kit; this helps the patch stick and means you don't lose the hole. Let all the air out of the tube again. Spread glue in a spiral out from the centre of the hole, making a glue patch that's generously bigger than the patch. This next step is the most important – let the glue dry completely. In average temperatures, this means five whole minutes. In the desert, you can wait two. If it's snowing, blow on the glue patch to keep it warm. Once the glue is dry, peel the foil off the back of the patch. Don't touch the rubber surface of the patch at all – use the clear plastic or paper to hold the patch. Drop it into place, then don't move it. Press it onto the tube with your hands. If it's very cold, clamp the patched part of the tube under your armpit to keep it warm enough for the glue to work, about another five minutes. You could peel the plastic or paper cover off next, but I normally leave it in place – it weighs nothing and saves you accidentally tearing off your neat patch. Refit the tube into the tyre before putting pressure into it because the newly-stuck patch is vulnerable and won't stick properly until it's trapped between tube and tyre under pressure. Puncture glue doesn't last long once the seal on the tube has been broken – it dries out in six months, however tightly you screw on the cap, so replace it regularly.

Valves

There are two types of bicycle valve: Presta and Schraeder. Presta is the thin one that road bikes always have. Schraeder is the fat car-type valve. Cheaper mountain bikes sometimes come fitted with car valves because they can be pumped up at gas stations. Presta valves are designed to work better at higher pressures and are more reliable – Schraeders leak if grit gets caught in them as you pump them up.

I always use Presta, but there is a bizarre law that says if you meet a stranger on the trail who's stuck because he can't fix his own puncture he will always have Schraeder valves, so you can't help him with your Presta pump. Luckily, most pumps now convert to fit either type of valve; with newer ones, you simply push any valve into the pump head and flick a switch. Many older ones require you to take the cover off the pump head and remove a small rubber grommet and a small plastic thing. Turn both parts over and refit them into the pump in the same order they came out – plastic first, then rubber. Refit the cap, tighten it hand-tight, and you're ready.

Schraeder inner tube/valve

Presta inner tube/valve

Suspension

Suspension used to be a luxury for cyclists, but it's become ubiquitous now. Yours will work much better if it's set up correctly and last a lot longer with a bit of basic cleaning and maintenance. Adjustments are very personal – they depend on your weight and riding style, so it's worth spending a little time fiddling to get the most out of your machine. This chapter also explains the meanings of some of the jargon that gets thrown around when people talk about suspension, making it seem much more mysterious than it actually is.

Fox Float rear suspension unit

Suspension: why you need it and how it works

Suspension technology is moving very quickly. What is currently state of the art is actually more likely to be part of a great work in progress than the final form. One happy result of this is that good, reliable designs constantly get cheaper and better. It's easy to forget how much better suspension forks are now than, say, six or seven years ago and to realize that for the same amount you paid for the fork back then, you can now get a whole bike with a better fork.

Many people originally resisted suspension forks – the extra weight was a high price to pay for the clunky suspension, which seemed to need an hour of servicing for every hour it was ridden. But even the early forks made bikes feel so much faster and helped them stick to the ground much better.

Although we now see fewer weird designs, radically different approaches continue to evolve, and there is no sign of suspension shaking down into just one clear "best design". In fact, sometimes the easiest way to tell what the next favourite design will be is by checking which one is currently being dismissed as outdated.

You would have thought that once we'd decided to fit suspension to bicycles, we could borrow the technology from other disciplines. But it didn't seem to work out like that. Although many of the best designers working on the problems come from other areas, like John Whyte from Formula One racing cars and Keith Bontrager from motocross, the bicycle seems to need to be thought about in different ways.

One reason is that the power source – the rider – has a low output and you can't just slap on a bigger engine. The other is that rider weight makes up a big proportion of the suspended weight, but that weight might vary considerably from one rider to another, even on the same sized bike.

Suspending disbelief

So, what does it all matter? You can hardly buy a decent mountain bike with rigid forks any more and full suspension goes up in quality and down in price all the time. All those people who used to say, "It's all very well for children, but it's so heavy you can't climb at all on it," used to be right. Early suspension was heavy and bounced so much when you climbed that you might as well be trying to hop up on a pogo stick. Some people are still saying this, but we can't hear them any more because we've left them behind at the bottom of the hill.

Full suspension is light enough to climb on now and good design means that full suspension helps you climb by keeping the back wheel pressed down into the ground, finding whatever grip there is to help you up hills. Suspension isn't just for people who want to jump off roofs – it allows you to blast over rough ground without carefully picking a line as you would with a rigid bike.

Suspension does need more care and attention than other parts of your bike. The first surprising thing is that when it's new, it needs attention right away. When you buy a new fork, or a new bike with forks and a rear shock, you need to spend a little time adjusting it.

The adjustments are very personal – nobody can set it up for you because adjustments must be done according to your weight and reaction speed.

It takes maybe upwards of half an hour – and you need to take your bike somewhere you can play safely without traffic. Follow the instructions in the sections on setting up your forks (page 146) and setting up your shocks (pages 155–156).

Once your suspension is set up correctly, check and clean it regularly – shocks don't respond at all to neglect. A check and clean needs no special tools and is easy to do, but it should be done regularly. There's no harm in checking shocks after every ride, but they also need a thorough inspection once a month.

Doing a full service on suspension forks and shocks is more advanced and often requires special tools particular to the make and model of your bike.

Previously, the instructions that came with forks were very comprehensive – manufacturers positively encouraged everybody to get in there and get dirty – but in the last few years there has been a clear move away from this.

Indeed, most manufacturers now take the opposite stance, with clear injunctions for you to not go further than the basic maintenance and regular inspection set out in the owner's manual.

However, your forks and shocks still have to be serviced frequently, so either go to your bike shop or send the fork or shock off to a shock specialist.

The same applies to rear shocks – you are expected to keep them clean and lubricated, but not to delve too deeply into their innards, as this will void your warranty.

Remember to increase the frequency of servicing if you ride in sandy, salty or muddy conditions, if you cover a lot of miles or if you have a reputation for breaking parts of your bicycle.

Part of the mystery of suspension is that talking about it demands all kinds of jargon: terms for the parts, for the adjustments and for how the fork reacts to the terrain.

Much confusion arises because most of the words have both a real-world meaning and a suspension-world meaning, which, while not altogether different, is a lot more precise.

Vital elements

Everybody claims their design is the best and most unique, but all suspension does the same job. A fork needs only two elements to work: a spring, which allows the wheel to move so you don't have to, and damping, which controls the speed at which the spring moves.

The spring can be a chamber of air, a coil spring, a rod of springy elastomers or a combination of all three. The spring performs the visible function – shock absorption. When you hit something the spring gets shorter, absorbing the pressure. The stiffness of the spring controls how far it moves when you hit something – a soft spring gives a lot; a stiff spring gives a little.

The more mysterious element is damping. Damping is vital because it controls the speed of the spring action. Pogo sticks are an example of springs with no damping – if you bounce on them, they keep bouncing.

This is great fun on a pogo stick but terrible on a bike. Damping controls the speed of the spring movement.

You may be able to control the speed of the damping with external knobs or it may be factory-set. More expensive forks allow you to control the speed of the fork compression separately from the speed at which the fork rebounds.

Learning the language of suspension: sag and preload

Your suspension is there to do a simple job – taking short, sharp shocks and turning them into smoother, more controllable forces. This allows you to travel fast over uneven terrain, while at the same time maintaining a reasonably level path, saving energy and allowing you to pick shorter, quicker lines on the trail.

Sag

Suspension moves up and down as you go over bumps and through potholes in the trail. Since the ideal is for your body to move in as straight a line as possible, ironing out the irregularities, it makes sense for the resting position of your suspension to be around the middle of its travel – so it can extend into dips as well as compressing over bumps. If the fork extends into dips so that you don't fall into them, you don't have to ride out of them, saving you some energy.

Sag is the distance that your fork or shock compresses when you sit still on your bike in your normal riding position. It's worked out by measuring the length of your fork or shock with and without you on the bike, then subtracting one number from the other. This tells you how much your weight has compressed the fork or shock.

The amount your forks compress when you sit on the bike depends partly on how much you weigh and partly on the geometry of the bike, so it needs to be set up individually for each person on his own bike. For those who can't be bothered to measure and adjust, new forks and shocks are supplied preset with an average amount of sag, but your suspension will work much better when tailored to you and your bike.

Each suspension fork manufacturer recommends an ideal amount of sag for your particular fork. There's no hard-and-fast rule, and suggested starting points range from 10 to 40 per cent of your total travel.

You also need to take into account what kind of ride you want – if you race, you set your forks up with a little less sag to minimize the amount of energy lost bobbing up and down. If you ride all day, you set them up with slightly more sag so your bike is comfortable to ride, absorbing trail noise so you don't get as tired. Rougher trails need still more sag and, if you jump around, you set your forks soft to absorb the force of landing.

Preload

This is the adjustment you make to the spring to alter the amount of sag. Increasing preload by pumping air into an air spring or compressing a coil spring will make the spring stiffer, keeping you higher in the air – less sag. Reducing pressure in an air spring or unwinding the preload on a coil spring reduces the sag and sits you lower down.

Altering the preload is the single most important adjustment to make on your forks or suspension because it sets the fork or shock up to match your weight and bike geometry. Coil springs will keep their adjustment once you've set it, but air spring forks tend to leak slowly, so they need to be checked every couple of months. You need a shock pump to measure and adjust the air pressure.

Learning the language of suspension: the spring thing

The spring in your fork is in many ways the simplest component – when you compress the fork, the spring resists the compressing and it re-extends the fork as soon as you release the compressing force.

Air springs, coil springs, elastomers

It may be freely available, light and highly adjustable, but air can be pesky because it doesn't like being trapped inside the fork. The fork manufacturer has to spend your money ensuring it doesn't leak. An air spring works by trapping air in a chamber at the top of the fork leg. As you compress the fork (by riding into an obstacle), you squash the air into an even smaller space, which it resists, responding by pushing out the fork again to make more space for itself and acting like a spring.

Coil springs are very simple and neither leak nor get affected by temperature. But if you want to drastically change their springiness, you either have to buy a new one or exchange it. If you buy a bike or a fork with a coil spring, make sure it's the right stiffness when you buy it by checking that you can adjust the sag for your weight. You can tune in a small amount of stiffness by altering the preload, but you can't make major changes – the spring has to be the right stiffness from the beginning. Exchanging steel springs for titanium ones is expensive but saves a little weight.

Elastomers used to be the most common spring type, but they have been largely superseded by coil springs. Elastomers are made of rods of urethane, usually in differently colours to denote their stiffness. Elastomers are a cheap spring medium, but their spring rate is affected by temperature, so they become much stiffer when cold and much softer when warm. Fine-tuning tricks for the first generation of elastomer-sprung forks included drilling holes across the elastomers to make them softer.

Your forks may have springs in both legs, but it's also common to have springs in one leg and a damping mechanism in the other. If there are springs in only one leg, they will almost always be in the left leg, nearest the disc brake. This keeps the damping mechanism farther away from the heat generated by the disc brake, which will affect the viscosity of the damping oil. Having springs in just one leg doesn't make the fork unbalanced – the two sides of the lower legs still work together as a unit. To get the best of both worlds, some forks use a combination of air and coil springs.

Spring rate

This is a measure of how much the suspension moves under pressure. Under the same force, a spring with a higher spring rate compresses less than one with a lower spring rate. If you are lighter you use a spring with a lower spring rate than someone heavier.

All suspension depends on the spring, either air or coil. One difference between air and coil spring forks is how they behave through their stroke. Coil spring forks are linear – that is, it takes roughly the same amount of force to compress the second half of the coil as it does to compress the first.

Air springs behave differently. As you compress the air chamber the air pressure increases, so you need progressively more force as you compress the fork – a progressive spring rate.

Learn the language of suspension: damping

Whenever you hit a bump, your fork and rear shock (or both) compress, absorbing the shock. When you've gone over the bump, they spring back out again, ready for the next bump. But you don't want them to spring out quickly and bounce you off your bike (if we wanted to play that game we'd return to rigid bikes), so we "damp" the movement by making the rebound extension happen more slowly than the original compression.

This is a good thing. However, you can take it too far. If the rebound happens too slowly, and you ride over a series of bumps, the fork compresses when you go over the first bump and will not have had time to extend again by the time you hit the second bump.

As you go over the series of bumps the fork gets shorter and shorter until you're riding on a very short rigid fork. This is called "stacking up" and can be avoided by reducing your rebound damping. Damping adjustment affects your steering too – forcing your front wheel around a corner compresses your fork and, if you have too much damping, the fork stays compressed through the turn, tucking under the handlebars rather than helping to turn.

Suspension forks are designed so that you can control the speed of the movement, adjusting the damping to find the middle ground between too fast and too slow. At the ideal setting your fork is always ready to respond to fresh forces, but it never moves more quickly than you can, so that you're always in charge. Ideal damping setting is an individual preference.

Once the fork is fully compressed, the springs start doing their job and act to force the fork to extend again. In order for the fork to re-extend, the oil has to pass back through

the holes in the piston – once more, only as fast as the oil will flow through the holes. The key to effective damping is controlling the speed of the oil through the holes. This is done by changing the thickness of the oil – see the oil weight section opposite – or more easily by changing the size of the oil-flow hole. A bigger hole equals faster oil flow equals less damping.

Turning the damping adjustment knobs on your forks will open or close the oil ports, changing the speed at which the oil can pass through the piston, so altering the speed at which your forks can respond to shocks.

Ideally, we'd like to control the movement of the oil through the holes separately in each direction, so that we can alter the rebound speed without affecting the compression speed. One way to do this is by mounting a thin, flexible washer on one side of the piston so that it covers a set of relatively large piston holes. When you hit a big bump the fork compresses, pushing oil through the piston towards the washer. The force bends the washer out of the way, allowing the oil to flow freely. Once the spring begins to re-extend the fork, the direction of oil flow is reversed. From this side the pressure of the oil will flatten the washer against the piston, blocking the holes and preventing oil flow. The addition of the washer means the piston acts like a turnstile, allowing free flow of oil in one direction and not in the other. However, you don't want to block the flow of oil completely, as this would simply lock the forks out. So a smaller hole is set in the middle of the piston where it won't get blocked by the washer. This allows the oil to flow back, but it does so much more slowly.

Rebound damping

After the preload adjuster, the most common adjustment that you'll find on forks is a rebound adjuster that controls the speed at which the fork re-extends after it's been squashed by hitting an obstacle. Here's an example of a rebound adjusting mechanism – this piston sits inside the fork stanchion. The rebounding oil is forced to flow through the hole in the damping shaft. The size of this hole is controlled by turning the rebound damping knob, which pushes a rod up through the centre of the shaft, gradually closing off the hole to reduce oil flow, thereby increasing the damping and slowing down the fork.

Piston

Hole in damping shaft

◀ Damping shaft

Compression damping

Compression damping affects how quickly the suspension responds to being compressed – if there is very little damping, the suspension reacts to every bump, which is good, but will reach the end of its travel very quickly, bottoming out when you hit something big. The damping in forks is often controled by damping oil being forced through a small hole as the fork compresses. A larger hole – or thinner oil – allows the fork to compress more quickly.

All forks have some kind of compression damping. As they get more expensive this is more likely to be externally adjustable. The compression damping mechanism can also be used to lock out (turn off) the fork or shock, so it doesn't bob when you climb. Turning the lockout knob closes the hole through which the oil passes, stopping the fork compressing. This design almost always "blows" – automatically releases if it's put under a lot of pressure – if you forget to turn off the lockout and hit something big.

Oil weight

Oil doesn't like being forced through small holes and the thicker it is, the less it likes it. So you can change the speed at which the fork moves, by making the oil thicker or by changing the size of the holes. The thickness of the oil is called its weight (wt). Thicker (gloopier) oil, say 15wt, is more reluctant to pass through small holes, and so increases the rebound damping. Thinner oil is lighter, say 5wt. This makes your forks faster. However, each fork is made for a specific weight, and changing the performance of the fork by altering the weight is a precise science. It's easier to use the rebound damping adjuster knob on your forks, which controls the size of the holes that the oil passes through.

Front suspension

Fork servicing isn't magic. It isn't even difficult, but it does need care and patience. It often needs very specific parts, which usually have to be ordered – there must be at least a million different spare suspension part numbers out there now. Don't assume you'll get spare parts for older forks. Some companies stock a longer back catalogue than others, but if your forks are more than about three years old, you're on shaky ground. That counts from when they were first made, so if you picked them up as a cheap end-of-line model, you'll arrive in obsolete land even sooner.

Forks are generally harder to repair than to maintain – once something goes wrong or breaks, they need special parts and usually special tools as well. This is often best left to your bike shop or the fork manufacturer. If your bike shop doesn't do fork repairs, you can send your forks off to be serviced (consult your local bike shop or the internet for a list of suppliers).

There are several designs of fork – air spring forks and coil spring forks being the main division. There isn't space here to go through a complete strip-down of every kind of fork, so I've included just a couple of examples if you're tackling this job.

The main reference text is always the owner's manual. If you don't have the one your fork came with, print a new one off the Internet. Make sure you get exactly the right year and model – even if the fork looks the same, small details change from one year to the next.

How far should you go? Use the manual for guidance – be aware that stripping down your fork further than recommended may invalidate the warranty.

Take extra care with any fork that uses an air spring. Always be sure to release all the air pressure from the fork before you take anything apart. This is easy to forget but crucial – start undoing things under pressure, and they rocket off. If they don't hit and hurt you, you'll probably lose something vital.

You should be able to service forks while they're on the bike, but you'll probably find it easier if you remove them. Follow the instructions on pages 170-173 – and you might as well service the headset while you're there. Either way, you'll need to be able to clamp the forks upright to add oil to the tops and to inject oil horizontally into the bottoms of the fork legs.

The most important constant maintenance for forks consists of only three things:

◆ Keep them clean, but don't jet-hose them. The most common cause of death for forks is dirt that works in between stanchions and seals, leaving scratches.

◆ Be conscious as you ride of any changes in the ride characteristic – nothing trashes forks faster than being used when something is a little loose.

◆ Ride them regularly. Forks get cantankerous if they're not ridden for a while.

There are two good reasons why people should carry out mild maintenance on their bikes more often than most do.

The first is simply economic: the more expensive forks are to buy, the more expensive they are to fix. Catch a problem sooner rather than later and you save yourself money.

The second reason is safety. Suspension is good at keeping your wheels on the ground, maximizing your grip and steering, but if

parts work loose and break free, you can be left with no control over your bike.

The very best time to clean your forks is just after your last ride, not just before your next one! Forks left dirty do not last as long as forks cleaned between rides. Find something wrong and you have time to fix it before going out next.

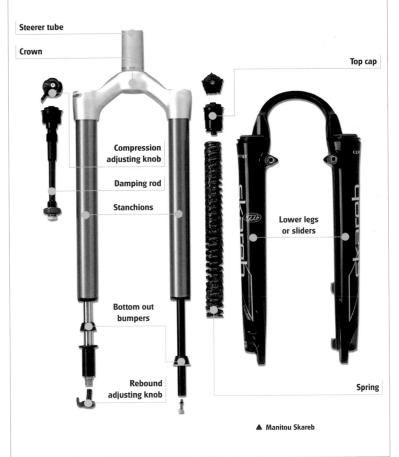

Steerer tube

Crown

Top cap

Compression adjusting knob

Damping rod

Stanchions

Lower legs or sliders

Bottom out bumpers

Rebound adjusting knob

Spring

▲ **Manitou Skareb**

Setting up your forks properly

I still get shocked by how many people spend a chunk of cash buying a new set of forks but can't find an hour to set them up properly. It's not hard and it makes an expensive fork ride like an expensive fork.

Basic forks allow you to set the preload, which you use to alter the sag. As forks get more expensive, you will also be able to adjust the rebound damping, the compression damping – the travel – and to temporarily lock out the forks to make them rigid. Different manufacturers put the controls in different places. Before you go any further, dig out your owner's manual for your fork, identify the adjustments you can make on it and locate where the adjusters are.

When setting up and tuning your forks, it's important to change just one thing at a time, so that you can see what effect you're having. If you have both front and rear suspension, set up the forks first, then set up the back end to match.

Sag

First set up the sag, which is where the fork compresses a little under your weight. The best information about how much sag your fork needs should come from your owner's manual. As a general guideline, start with 20–25 per cent of your total fork travel for cross-country forks and 30–35 per cent for downhill/freeride forks.

This is only a rough guide; your fork is designed for a specific amount of sag. Pages 147–149 guide you through setting up your fork sag; pages 155-156 describe setting up your shock sag.

Rebound damping

Once the sag is sorted, adjust the rebound damping. You'll need to take your bike outside and ride around for this bit. People like to lean on suspension forks, watch them spring back and nod knowledgeably, but there's no substitute for getting out and seeing how your fork reacts to being properly ridden.

Most manufacturers have a pretty good idea of a starting point for you and will recommend it in the manual. I like to set my rebound damping as fast as I can before it's so fast that the bars come back up quicker than I do. I think that's the key – to match the fork's reaction speed to yours. The faster it is, the less often it gets caught out by a series of bumps, hitting the next before recovering from the last. But it's a very personal adjustment. Your rebound damping setting affects the bike's feel when cornering – if you have too much rebound damping, the fork stays compressed as you turn, digging the wheel into the corner rather than pushing you around it.

Find a baby dropoff that you can ride over repeatedly – 10cm (4 inches) or so is about right. Set your fork to the slowest rebound damping position (i.e. maximum damping equals slowest movement), and ride over the dropoff. Reset to the fastest damping position (least damping equals fastest movement), and ride off again. You'll feel your bike react differently, with the handlebars springing straight back towards you.

Repeat the dropoff, slowing the rebound damping down a little at a time – if your adjuster has distinct clicks, go one click at a time. You're aiming to find a position where you're completely in control throughout the cycle of the fork, but with as little damping as possible.

Once you've found the right place, write down the adjustment so that you can find it again. I use a marker pen to draw a line on the fork and the knob, so that I can find the adjustment again by lining up the two marks.

Compression damping

If you have a compression damping adjustment, set this last. This adjustment affects how fast your fork compresses when it hits an obstacle. Again the right setting is tied to your reaction speed. If you set up the preload correctly and are still bottoming out, you don't have enough compression damping. If the fork doesn't respond to small obstacles, you have too much compression damping.

With many forks your compression damping is preset and cannot be adjusted. I don't think this is a great loss, I've always found the preset levels to be fine.

If you have both front and rear suspension, set up the front forks first, then set the back end to match. Set yourself a time and place where you can ride safely without looking where you're going, ideally somewhere fairly flat with a single obstacle you can ride over repeatedly without too much effort. You need to ride over the identical object a number of times to see the effect the adjustments are having.

Setting your sag

Use the steps below to measure your sag and adjust the preload to the recommended sag. Remember, this is just a starting point though.

Once you've followed the steps, ride your bike to see how it feels. If you hit something hard, you'll go all the way through the travel of the fork to the point where the top part thuds against the bottom part. This is

"bottoming out the fork". It's not a bad thing – if you don't ever hit that point during normal riding, you aren't using all the available fork travel. Play with the initial sag setting to aim to bottom out about once a ride.

SETTING YOUR SAG

◀ **Step 1:** Work out your travel. If it's written in your owner's manual, use that measurement. Manuals for air shocks often give you a recommended air pressure for your weight, but it's worth testing the actual sag you get on your bike because it depends on your position on the bike and the configuration of your shock.

◀ **Step 2:** If you don't have the manual, work travel out like this: with the fork fully extended measure the distance from the bottom of the fork crown to the top of the lower leg seal, i.e. check how much stanchion is showing.

◀ **Step 3:** Release air pressure in air forks or remove coil springs in coil forks and push the fork right down as far as it will go. Measure the same distance again. Take the second number from the first. This is your total travel. Replace coil springs, reinflate air chambers.

◀ **Step 4:** Take a ziptie and loop it around one of your fork stanchions so it's fairly tight but can still be pushed up and down easily. Push it down so it sits just above the seal.

◀ **Step 5:** Lean your bike against a wall and mount it carefully. Sit still on the bike in your normal riding position. Don't bounce up and down. Get off the bike. Your weight on the bike has compressed the forks, pushing up the ziptie. Now measure the distance between the ziptie and the top of the seal. This is the sag.

◀ **Step 6:** Adjust the air pressure or the coil-spring preload until the sag is the required proportion of the total travel.

Toolbox

- **Tape measure**
- **Instruction book for your forks** – if you haven't got the original instructions, download a replacement from the internet; make sure you get the right model and year
- **Air shocks** – a shock pump: almost all forks, and all shocks, use the universal Schrader fitting. However, there are a couple of anomalies which require a special valve adapter, including some Marzocchi forks. These come supplied with the fork, but you can get replacements from their distributor if you lose yours

Inspecting and maintaining your forks

Regular, careful fork maintenance will save you money –
keeping your forks clean will help reduce servicing frequency.
It's also a good time to inspect them, allowing you to pick up and
sort out potential problems quickly.

All fork maintenance starts with a good clean.
Disconnect the V-brakes and drop the wheel
out of the frame, so that you can get to the
forks properly. For disc brakes, push a wedge
of clean cardboard between the disc pads, so
that you don't accidentally pump the brake
pads out of the callipers. Go through the
steps below; if you find worn or broken
components, it's time for a fork service. Don't
ride damaged forks – they may let you down
without warning.

◆ Start by washing the lower legs,
stanchions and fork crown. Plain water
is fine, although if they're really grimy,
use Finish Line or other similar bike
cleaners.

◆ As you wash the dirt off, inspect the
forks carefully and methodically. Start
with dropouts. Check for cracks around
the joint between the fork leg and the
dropout, inside and out.

◆ Take a look at the condition of the
surfaces that your wheels clamp onto,
inside and out. These grip the axle and
stop the wheel popping out of the fork.
The serrations on the quick-release and
axle make dents in the fork – make
sure that these are clean, crisp dents,
rather than worn craters that indicate
the wheel has been shifting about.

◆ Check each fork leg in turn. You're
looking for splits, cracks or dents. Big

dents will weaken the fork, and prevent
the stanchion from moving freely inside
the lower legs. Cracks and dents both
mean that it's new fork time.

◆ Take a look at disc and V-brake mounts.
Check disc mounts for cracks and check
that all calliper fixing bolts are tight.

◆ Check the bolts at the bottoms of the
fork legs – these hold everything
together, so make sure they're not
working loose. Look for signs that oil has
been leaking out from under the bolts.

◆ Clean muck out from behind the
brake arch – grit has a tendency to
collect here.

◆ Inspect the wipers that clean the
stanchions as they enter the lower legs.
Tears or cuts will allow grit into the
wipers, where they will scour your
stanchions. The tops of the wipers are
usually held in place with a fine circular
spring that should sit in the lip at the
top of the wiper.

◆ Check the stanchions. If grit gets stuck
in the wipers or seals, it will be
dragged up and down as your fork
cycles, wearing vertical grooves in the
forks. These grooves in turn provide a
new route in for more dirt.

◆ Check all the adjuster knobs. They often
stick out so that you can turn them
easily, but this does make them
vulnerable.

◆ Refit the wheel and reconnect the V-brakes. Pull the front brake on and hold one of the stanchions just above the lower leg. Rock the bike gently back and forth. You may be able to feel a little bit of flex in the forks, but you should not be able to feel the lower legs knocking. Lots of movement here means you need new bushings.

◆ Push down firmly on the bars, compressing the forks. They should spring back smoothly when you release the bars. If they stutter or hesitate returning, it's time for a fork service.

◆ Finally, finish off by polishing the lower legs. It makes the forks look better, which is important in itself, but also leaves a waxy finish that means dirt doesn't stick so well to the fork.

Wipers/seals

Stanchions

V-brake Mounts

Lower legs

Disc mounts

Dropouts

▶ **Marzocchi MX Comp**

Rear suspension

Mountain biking – being highly competitive in sporting, technology and commercial terms – boasts as many different rear suspension designs as it does bike companies. And each proud designer knows their beautiful baby blows the others away. While the models differ in detail, it is possible to divide the majority into three types: cantilever, linkage and URT (unified rear triangle). All three rise and fall in popularity over time. Within each type, there are bikes that have been designed with computer-aided whatsits and cutting-edge doodahs but still ride like dogs. Meanwhile, those you heard a convincing argument against last week still feel fast and furious.

Choosing a suspension bike can be stressful. Anybody with any experience has an opinion on what suspension you should consider and each one is different. However, out there is a bike designed by someone who wants the same from a ride as you do. My advice is try to ride as many different designs as you can before making a decision.

The appropriate design for you depends on your build and riding style. Some people sit in the saddle as long as possible, using their energy economically (they might have a road-bike background). They may generally dislike designs where the position of the rear end affects the chain length, snapping back as they pedal. Others, maybe with a BMX or trail bike background, are up and out of the saddle with little excuse, using their shoulders and their body weight rather than their legs to propel the bike. They may waste loads of energy, but they like great short bursts of power.

Rear suspension design has two elements: frame shape and shock characteristic. All frames are based on the principle that the rear part of the frame is hinged so that the rear wheel moves relative to the main body of the frame. A lot of thought goes into manipulating the pivot and strut positions that

make up the rear end in order to control the axle path or the position of the axle relative to the frame as it moves through its travel.

Trail forces come from different directions. When you land from a dropoff you apply force directly upwards and, if this were the only force on the rear wheel, the equation would be much simpler. But you're also driving the back wheel by pedalling, applying force to the wheel along the horizontal and along the chain from chainring to sprocket.

If the hinge between the back and front of the bike lies between the chainset and the rear axle, then pedalling activates the suspension. The movement of the rear end as it reacts to the terrain causes movement in the pedals – "chain reaction." This isn't always a bad thing; in climbing, the pedalling tends to extend the suspension and dig the back wheel into the ground, giving you extra grip. Chain reaction is not so alarming, as long as it isn't huge. Your feet get familiar with dealing with the effect quickly, until you don't notice it. Successful suspension design makes the rear axle as responsive as possible to uneven terrain, while minimizing the extent to which pedalling compresses the shock and wastes your energy.

Suspension: measuring travel

Travel is the total distance your suspension unit can move. More travel means that your shock unit can absorb larger shocks, stretching out the short, sharp impacts so that you can maintain control over your bike. Longer travel allows people to do stuff on bikes that would never have been possible five years ago.

Longer travel isn't all good, though. Frames have to be beefier and heavier to maintain stiffness, as well as to withstand abuse. The shape of a long travel frame changes through the travel, making it tiring to ride long distances or to take on steep climbs. Cross-country frames with a medium amount of travel seek to find a compromise between soaking up uneven terrain, maximizing grip by keeping the rear wheel glued to the ground, and providing a comfortable, stable pedalling platform. Microtravel suspension – where the rear triangle moves 5cm (2 inches) or so – will absorb harsh trails, adding a bit of comfort with the minimum of weight penalty.

Like front suspension, rear shocks need to be set up so that when you sit on the bike the suspension settles slightly. This is

important – it means that your rear wheel can drop down into dips, as well as fold upwards to pass over lumps and obstacles in your path. This keeps you floating in a horizontal straight line, rather than climbing in and out of every irregularity on the trail, saving you energy.

Each manufacturer has their own ideas about how much of your total travel should be taken up by this initial sag, so you'll need to consult the shock handbook or the manufacturer's website to find out their recommendations.

Since the sag is always given as a proportion of total travel, you'll need to know the travel as well before you can start setting your sag. If you don't know it already, use the steps below to measure it.

MEASURING TOTAL TRAVEL

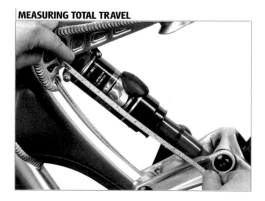

◀ **Step 1:** Stand the bike up and measure the distance from centre to centre between the shock eyelets. This is the extended length.

◀ **Step 2:** Release the spring: for an air shock, take the valve cap off, push down the pin in the middle of the valve, pump the bike up and down a couple of times and push the pin down again to release the rest of the air. For coil shocks, back off the preload-adjuster, as far as it will go, so that the spring dangles loose.

◀ **Step 3:** Push the bike down to compress the shock and measure the distance between the eyelets again. Subtract the second measurement from the first and that's your total available travel.

Shock pumps

These sometimes, but not always, come with a new shock. Very occasionally, they will also come supplied with a new bike that has an air shock. Mostly, you'll have to buy yourself a separate one. Shock pumps have a narrower barrel than normal pumps, to allow you to put very small but accurate quantities of air into your shock and an integral pressure gauge. They always let a little air out from the shock into the pump when you attach them, so the reading you get straight away off the pump won't be an accurate pressure reading.

Setting up sag

Once you've worked out how much travel your bike has, put a small amount of air back in the shock or remount the coil and put in a single turn of preload.

The next step is to calculate how much sag you're aiming to have. Different bike shapes and shock models work best with different amounts of sag, but as a rule, for cross-country racers it's 15–25 per cent of total travel; for general cross-country, it's 20–30 per cent; and for downhill/freeride, it's 30–35 per cent. These are guidelines only – refer to your shock manual for recommendations. This gives you a starting point to use to tune to your preferences. Don't worry about that now, we take that into account at the test stage. Now work out what sag you would like.

Coil shock

You'll need a friend to help you with this. Measure the distance between the shock mounting bolts. Sit on your bike in your normal riding position – it helps to lean against a wall for this – and get your friend to measure the same distance again between the centres of the shock eyelets. Subtract this new measurement from the original unloaded shock length and you have the sag. If the amount is more than you expected, add preload to the coil spring. If it's less than you expected, back off the coil spring until you have it about right.

Air springs are adjustable throughout the range of what you need, but coil springs have a much narrower range.

For example, Fox Vanilla springs are designed for up to two turns of the preload-adjusting ring. Crank them up too much and they won't work properly. Leave them too loose and they bang around. Ideally, with the exact spring rate, you shouldn't need to use preload at all. If you can't get the adjustment

you need from the spring you have, get a softer or a harder spring. Give the bike shop the details of your bike (make, model and year) and spring (spring rate and travel as printed on the spring), as well as your weight, so that they can work out the correct spring for you.

Air shock

You can work out the sag on an air shock without pressuring an assistant to measure for you – the travel O-ring on the shock shaft will get pushed down as you compress the shock and will then remain there when the shock re-extends, making it simple to measure how far you squashed the shock by sitting on the bike. See page 156 for details. You'll need a shock pump to add air and to measure the pressure inside the shock.

Your shock may leak slowly over time – some leak faster than others – so you will need to recheck the sag regularly. But if you find yourself having to top up the shock more than once a month or so, it's time to send your shock off to a service centre for some fresh seals.

10% sag – total travel divided by 10

15% sag – total travel divided by 7

20% sag – total travel divided by 5

25% sag – total travel divided by 4

33% sag – total travel divided by 3

AIR SHOCK

◀ **Step 1:** For air shocks, push the travel O-ring right up the shaft of the shock, so that it rests against the air sleeve.

◀ **Step 2:** Sit in your normal position on the bike in normal riding clothes. Just sit, don't bounce or twiddle. Get off the bike. Your weight will have compressed the shock, pushing the travel O-ring along the shaft. Measure the gap between the air sleeve and the O-ring. This is your sag.

◀ **Step 3:** If the measurement is less than you expected, release a little air from the shock. If it's more than you expected, add a little air – screw the shock pump onto the valve, enough so that you can hear a little air escaping then half a turn more. Add a little pressure. Remove the shock pump, and test again. Make a note of what pressure you ended up with!

Testing and adjusting rebound damping for the best setting

If you don't have this adjustment, it doesn't mean you don't have rebound damping, but rather that the manufacturer has decided what works best and they don't want you fiddling with it.

First, get a feeling for the effect of the rebound damping adjustment before finding the right setting. Find a place where you can repeat a simple five-minute loop – nothing special, a parking lot will do fine. Ride the loop twice at the two extremes of the rebound damping adjustment to get a feel for the effect of changing the settings. Then set the rebound damping in the central position; for example, if it has a total 12 clicks, start with six clicks.

Find a clear, flat space without cars with a single baby dropoff – 50mm (2 inches) or 100mm (4 inches) or so – to ride repeatedly. The idea is you ride over the dropoff, the shock compresses, rebounds further than it started from and returns to its original position. If the shock springs back and kicks you on landing, the rebound is too fast and you need to increase the damping. If you wallow on landing, it's too slow and needs to be reduced. At first you may want to make radical changes to the adjustment to learn its effect. Whatever you do, remember to keep a clear and constant note of all changes you make and resist the temptation to fiddle randomly with combinations – if playing with the rebound damping, leave the sag alone.

Now for the test ride. Go out and play. You should bottom out the shock about once every ride. If not, you are not using the full travel, which is a waste. Play with the sag, a little at a time. This is where your personal taste and riding style come into play. If you stand a lot, up and out of the saddle, you may prefer a stiffer ride at the lower end of your recommended sag range.

Maintaining rear suspension

Rear shocks have two levels of servicing: they need to be kept clean; and the moving parts need regular lubrication. The bushings that allow them to move must be kept clean and must be replaced when worn. They need to be checked regularly to ensure they're working properly. You can kill a shock very quickly by continuing to ride when something internal is broken.

Rear shocks often sit directly in the firing line for mush thrown up by your back wheel and their performance deteriorates quickly if you ignore them. Conversely, keep them clean and greased and they last a whole lot longer.

Deeper, internal servicing and tuning must be carried out by a shock servicer. Depending on make the internal parts may be filled with nitrogen or under high pressure. Don't get involved. It's too easy to hurt yourself and the action voids the warranty. Send the shock to the service centre.

Luckily there are enough specialists to do the job and, luckily again, once you've taken the shock off the bike, it is small enough to send easily. One thing you can do to help this process is to clean up the shock before despatching it.

It is cleaned at the other end, but it's polite to wipe off last weekend's fun before putting it in a box. The correct service centre depends on the make of shock.

Bottom brackets and headsets

These are the two main bearings that keep your pedals turning and allow you to steer your bicycle. They both get unfairly ignored too often. Bottom brackets can be replaced with a minimum of tools. Headset replacement is a job for your bike shop but regular servicing of the bearings is much simpler – since A-headsets have replaced the older threaded headsets, it can usually be done with one or two Allen keys.

Headset bearings allow your forks to rotate freely in your frame

Creaking noises

This kind of noise from the bottom bracket area can spoil a good ride. Like all creaking sounds, investigate it right away – bicycles rarely complain unless something is loose, worn or about to snap. If your bicycle is giving you warning creaks, it's worth paying heed.

Fat-tubed aluminium bikes amplify the smallest sound. Anything with any tube fatter than you can get your hand around is, basically, a soundbox. Try these silencing measures and then test to see if the creaking has gone away. If nothing works, note that frames transmit noises strangely, so creaks can sound as if they come from somewhere else. Common causes include handlebar and stem bolts as well as rear hubs.

SORTING OUT NOISES

◀ **Step 1:** Tighten both crank bolts clockwise. They both need to be tight – you will need a long (at least 200mm [8 inch]) Allen key, not just a multi-tool. The 8mm Allen key on multi-tools is for emergencies only.

◀ **Step 2:** If that doesn't work, remove both crank bolts, grease the threads and under the heads and refit firmly.

◀ **Step 3:** Tighten both pedals. Remember that the left-hand pedal has a reverse thread – see the pedals section, which starts on page 179, for more details.

◀ **Step 4:** Remove both pedals, grease the threads and refit firmly. This sounds farfetched but it does the trick more often than you'd imagine. Dirt or grit on the pedal threads will also cause creaking, so clean the threads on the pedal and inside the crank.

◀ **Step 5:** Take hold of each pedal and twist it. The pedal should not move on its own axle. If it does, it could well be the source of the creak and needs stripping and servicing (see the pedals section). Spray a little light oil, like GT85, on the cleat release mechanism. Don't use chain oil – it's too sticky and will pick up dirt.

◀ **Step 6:** Remove the crank and chainset, loosen the left-hand bottom bracket cup, tighten the right-hand cup firmly (remember it has a reverse thread), then tighten the left-hand cup (normal thread). Refit crank and chainset and tighten bolts firmly.

Removing and refitting cranks

Start on the left-hand side of the bike. Remove the Allen key bolt (8 or 10mm) or 14mm bolt that holds the crank on.

Remove washers from the crank and look into the hole to check the kind of axle. If the bike is an older or entry-level one, you will see the square end of the axle. On newer bikes, you see the round end of a splined axle. Use the appropriate crank extractor – splined axles are fatter, so an older crank extractor, designed for square taper cranks, cannot push out the axle. Crank extractors for splined axles have a fatter head, so do not fit older square cranks.

REMOVING A CRANK

◀ **Step 1:** Step 1: The crank bolts should be tightly fitted, so you will need a long Allen key (or 14mm socket) to undo the bolt. If you find the bolts come off without too much effort, tighten them more firmly next time!

◀ **Step 2:** Hold the handle, or the nut end of the inner part of the tool and turn the outer part of the tool. You will see that turning one against the other means that the inner part of the tool moves in or out of the outer part.

◀ **Step 3:** Next, back off the inner part of the tool so that its head disappears inside the outer part of the tool.

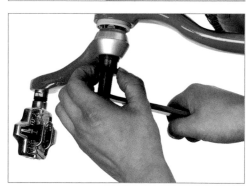

◀ **Step 4:** Thread the outer part of the tool into the threads in the crank that you've revealed by taking off the bolt. The crank is soft in comparison to the tool so take care not to crossthread the tool and damage the crank, which will be expensive. Thread on the tool as far as it will go.

◀ **Step 5:** Start winding in the inner part of the tool. It will move easily at first, but will then meet the end of the axle and stiffen. You need to be firm with it. Once it starts moving, turning the tool gets easier as it pushes the axle out of the crank.

◀ **Step 6:** Once you've started the crank moving on the axle, the crank will come off in your hand. Pull it off the axle and remove the tool from the crank.

The crank extractor has two parts. The outer part threads onto the crank; the inner part threads through the outer part and bears on the end of the axle.

As long as the outer part is firmly fitted into the crank, as you thread in the inner part, it pushes the axle off the crank.

The inner part of the tool will either have an integral handle, like the Park one in the picture on this page, or it will have separate flats for a spanner. Either version works fine.

If at any time the outer part of the tool starts to pull out of the chainset, stop

immediately. If you continue, you will strip the threads out of the chainset, and it will be difficult to remove the chainset without destroying it.

Remove the tool from the crank and check that you've removed all bolts and washers.

If there are any accidentally left in there, remove them and try again. If you can find no reason why the threads are stripping, this might be a good time to beat a retreat to your bike shop and get your mechanic to have a go.

Refitting the crank and chainset

The same procedure is used to fit both crank and chainset. Fit the chainset first. Before starting clean the axle and the hole in the chainset thoroughly. Make sure there's no dirt left on the tapers or between the splines, or you will get creaking. Apply antiseize to any titanium parts.

There are two different opinions about whether the axle should be greased before you fit the cranks onto it. Proponents on both sides of the discussion are often fiercely loyal to their points of view. The advantage of greasing the axle is that the lubrication allows the crank to be pulled further onto the axle, fitting it more tightly. Those who prefer not to grease the axle say that the grease layer allows the two surfaces to move against each other, leading to potential creaking and then allowing the parts to work themselves loose. Personally, I can be convinced by either argument, but have found that it makes more difference whether the axle and crank surfaces are clean than whether they are greased. New bottom brackets often come with antiseize already applied to the right-hand axle; this should be left on.

Inspect the surface of both the axle and the holes in the cranks. Square taper axles should be flat with no pitting. The crank hole is the place you're most likely place to find damage – the hole needs to be perfectly square and must fit smoothly over the axle. The most common problem is where loose cranks have rounded themselves off on the axle, smearing the shape of one or more of the corners of the square. Splined cranks will also be damaged by being ridden loose. Each spline should be crisp and clean. Replace damaged cranks immediately – they will never hold securely and will cause expensive damage to your bottom bracket axle.

Slide the chainset over the end of the axle. Line it up with the square or splined axle and push on it firmly. Grease the threads of the fixing bolts and add a dab of grease under the head of the bolt, which may otherwise creak. Fit the bolt and tighten firmly.

For the last part, line the crank up with the Allen key/socket spanner, so they are almost parallel. Hold one in each hand and stand in front of the chainset. With both arms straight use your shoulders to tighten the crank bolts. (This uses the strength of your shoulders and reduces the chance of stabbing yourself with the chainring if you slip.)

Next, fit the crank onto the other end of the bottom bracket axle. Line it up so that it points in the opposite direction to the one on the other side. The bike feels odd if you fit the crank to a neighbouring spline. Tighten that crank on firmly too.

◀ **Hold crank steady, retighten crank bolt firmly**

Aheadsets: adjusting bearings

The bearings are adjusted for no play at all, while allowing the fork and bars to rotate smoothly in the frame without resistance. Check the bearings as below; if they're tight, or there is play, adjust them. You wear your bearings really quickly if you ride them either tight or loose.

It's vital to check that your stem bolts are tight after finishing this job. Some people will tell you to leave your stem bolt slightly loose, so that in the event of a crash your stem will twist on the steerer tube rather than bending your handlebars. You should not do this. The consequences of your stem accidentally twisting on your steerer tube as you ride are far too serious and dangerous. Always tighten your stem bolts firmly. It is fine to slacken the topcap bolt off though – it's only needed for headset adjustment and can be a handy emergency bolt if something else snaps!

Checking the adjustment

A tight headset makes your steering feel heavy and wear quickly. A loose headset will make the bike rock and shudder as you brake.

Either situation will wear out your bearings quickly. To check the adjustment pick the bike up by the handlebars and turn the handlebars. The bars should turn easily and smoothly with no effort. You should not feel any notches.

Drop the bike back to the ground, and turn the bars 90 degrees, so the wheel points to one side. Hold on the front brake, to stop the wheel rolling, and rock the bike gently backwards and forwards in the direction the frame, not the wheel, is pointing. You should not feel or hear any knocking or play. Turning the bars sideways isolates headset play, avoiding confusion with any movement in your brake pivots or suspension. Sometimes it helps to hold the cups, above and below, while you rock the bike – you shouldn't feel any movement at all.

ADJUSTING AHEADSET BEARINGS

◀ **Step 1:** Loosen the stem bolt(s) so the stem can rotate easily on the steerer. Undoing the top cap makes the headset turn more easily; tightening it eliminates play. Approach the correct adjustment gradually, testing for rocking. It is easier to get the adjustment right by tightening a loose headset than by loosening a tight one.

◄ **Step 2:** If the headset is too tight, back off the topcap a few turns, hold the front brake and rock the bars gently back and forth. This frees up the headset bearings. Then gradually retighten the topcap, testing the adjustment constantly. Stop when all play is eliminated.

◄ **Step 3:** Once you have the adjustment correct, align the stem with the front wheel and firmly tighten the stem bolts. Check the stem is secure by holding the front wheel between your knees and twisting it. If you can turn it the stem bolts need to be tighter. Check the adjustment again and repeat if necessary – sometimes tightening the stem bolt shifts everything around.

Toolbox

Adjusting bearings:
- Allen keys to fit stem bolts and top cap
- Both of these are almost always a 5mm or 6mm Allen key, you may occasionally come across a 4mm Allen key fitting

Adjusting stem height:
- The same Allen keys as above, to fit your stem bolts and top cap

Servicing:
- Allen keys as above
- Tools to disconnect your brake cable, lever or disc calliper 4, 5 or 6mm Allen key
- Degreaser to clean bearing surfaces
- Quality grease – preferably waterproof
- Fresh bearings: ball bearings for headsets are generally 4mm ($\frac{5}{32}$ inch), but take old ones to a bike shop to match them up.

Aheadsets: stem height

If your handlebar is set at the correct height, you are more comfortable and your bike is more stable and easier to steer. You can change the height in a couple of ways.

Swapping the stem is easiest – you can change both the length of the stem and the height. Make minor changes to the height of the stem by swapping the position of the washers on it. If you take off your stem and remove a couple of washers from the steerer tube, your stem sits lower when you refit it. Replace the washers above the stem before refitting the top cap – they push the stem down the steerer tube when you tighten the top cap. You'll end up with a little stack of washers protruding above your stem.

ADJUSTING STEM HEIGHT

◀ **Step 1:** Remove the top cap. You'll need to undo the top cap bolt all the way and wiggle the cap off. This reveals that star-fanged nut inside the steerer tube. Lift off any washers that were sitting between the top cap and the stem. Check the condition of the top cap. If it's cracked or the recess where the bolt head sits is distorted, replace it.

◀ **Step 2:** Loosen the stem bolts so that the stem moves freely on the steerer tube. Pull the stem up and off – you may need to twist it a little to help it on its way. Tape the entire handlebar assembly to the top tube so that hoses and cables don't get kinked under the weight of the bars.

◀ **Step 3:** If you've hung the bike in a workstand, keep a hand on the forks so that they don't slide out of the headset. Add or remove washers from the stack under the stem. If you're adding washers, you can only add washers that came off above the stem.

◀ **Step 4:** Replace the stem, then any leftover washers – everything that came off the steerer tube should go back on. The washers are all necessary because, as you tighten the top cap, they push down onto the stem and then the bearings, adjusting the headset.

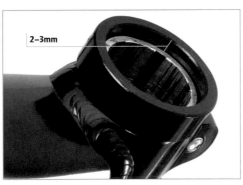

2–3mm

◀ **Step 5:** Check the height of the washer stack above the top of the steerer tube. There should be a gap of 2–3mm (around $\frac{1}{8}$ inch). This should be a single washer, not a stack of thinner ones as individual washers have a tendency to get caught and stop you adjusting the headset properly. Add or remove washers from the top of the stack to achieve the desired 2–3mm gap.

169

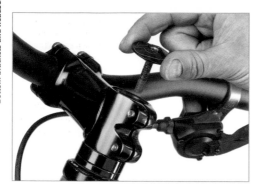

◀ **Step 6:** Replace the top cap, and go to "Aheadset: adjusting bearings" on page 166. Ensure the stem bolts are securely tightened.

Headsets: regular maintenance to ensure a smooth ride

Headsets are remarkably simple to service, needing no special tools at all, just one (or two) Allen keys, degreaser or other cleaning agent and good quality grease.

Headsets, like bottom brackets, are frequently ignored, gradually deteriorating without you noticing. Regular servicing will help keep them turning smoothly and will make your bike feel more responsive. Cleaning the dirt out and replacing the grease with fresh stuff will help make the bearing surfaces last as long as possible. With the ball type, it's worth replacing the bearings at every service – new ones only cost a few dollars. Cartridge bearings are more expensive and can usually be resuscitated with care. If you're replacing them, always take the old cartridge bearings along to your bike shop to match up new ones. The size and shape are crucial.

Check carefully for pitting once you've cleaned out the headset. Even very tiny pits are a sign that your headset needs replacing.

The surface that suffers most is the crown race, the ring at the very bottom of the headset that's attached to your forks. Your bearings will quickly wear a groove in this, showing you where they run. The crown race should be completely smooth. You should be able to run a fingernail around the groove without it catching in any blemishes on the surface.

Headset hints

Before you start, remove the front wheel. It helps a lot to disconnect the front brake as well – for cable brakes, disconnect the brake cable from the lever. For hydraulic systems, either remove the brake lever from the handlebars or the brake calliper from the forks. That way, you won't damage the cable or hose when you remove the forks.

SERVICING HEADSETS

◀ **Step 1:** Undo the Allen key on the very top of the stem, the top cap bolt. Remove the top cap completely, revealing the star-fanged nut inside the steerer tube. Undo the bolts that secure the stem while holding onto the forks and the stem should pull off easily.

◀ **Step 2:** Tape or tie the stem to the top tube out of the way (protect the frame paint with a cloth). Pull off any washers and set them aside. Pull the forks gently and slowly down out of the frame.

◀ **Step 3:** The fork may not want to come out. Lots of headsets have a plastic wedge that sits above the top bearing race and that sometimes gets very firmly wedged in place. Release it by sliding a small screwdriver into the gap in the plastic wedge and twist slightly to release the wedge. You could also try tapping the top of the fork with a plastic or rubber mallet.

◀ **Step 4:** Catch all pieces as they come off and note the orientation and order of bearing races and seals.

◀ **Step 5:** Once you've got the fork out, lay out all the bearing races and cups in order. Check the bearing cup at the bottom of the head tube for any bearings or seals left in there. Clean all the races carefully: the ones attached to the frame top and bottom; the loose one off the top chunk of bearings when the fork came out; and the crown race still attached to the fork.

◀ **Step 6:** Look carefully at the clean races and check for pits or rough patches. Pitted bearing races mean a new headset. This needs special tools and so is a job for your bike shop. Otherwise, clean all the bearings and seals. Grease the cups in the frame enough that the bearings sit in grease up to their middles. Cartridge bearings just need a thin smear to keep the weather out.

◀ **Step 7:** Don't grease the crown race on the fork or the loose top head race. Fit a bearing ring into the cups at either end of the head tube and replace the seals. The direction the races face is crucial, so replace them facing the same direction they were. Slide the fork back through the frame and slide the loose top race back down over the steerer tube.

◀ **Step 8:** If it had a plastic wedge, put it next, followed by any washers or covers in the order they came off. Refit the stem and any washers from above the stem. Push the stem firmly down the steerer tube.

2–3mm

◀ **Step 9:** Make sure there's a gap of 2–3mm (around $\frac{1}{8}$ inch) between the top of the steerer tube and the top of the stem, adding or removing washers if necessary. Refit the top cap, then adjust bearings (see page 166). Tighten the stem bolts securely, then refit your brake lever or cable and your front wheel. Check your stem is tight and facing forwards. Check front brake.

Components

When you buy a new bike, the manufacturer makes guesses about what size and shape you'll be, and chooses the "finishing kit" – handlebars, stem, seatpost and saddle – accordingly. These are personal items though and getting the right size and shape, adjusted to fit you, makes a big difference to how comfortable your ride is. Correct fit also determines how efficiently you travel. This chapter also includes a guide to servicing pedals and doubling the lifespan of your bearings.

fi´zi:k pavé saddle, USE seat post

Seatposts

Seatposts must be sized very accurately: the 30 different common sizes are sized in increments of 0.2mm. One size too big won't fit your frame; one size too small will fit but rock slightly at every pedal stroke, slowly destroying your frame. If you have your old seatpost, the right size is stamped on it. If in doubt, get your bike measured at the shop.

All seatposts have a minimum insertion line. This is usually indicated by a row of vertical lines printed or stamped near the bottom of the seatpost. The vertical lines must always be inside the frame.

If you have to lift your seatpost high enough to see the marks, you need either a longer seatpost or a bigger bike. In the unlikely event that you have no markings on your seatpost, you need a length at least 2.5 times the diameter of the post inside the frame. Seatposts that are raised too high will snap your frame.

Suspension frames with an interrupted seat tube may need a shorter seatpost, which will not bang on the shock at the bottom of its travel.

Seatpost failures

One common reason for seatpost failure is the clamp bolt shearing. Luckily, this will usually warn you by creaking as it begins to work loose. Any movement between the saddle and the seatpost needs immediate attention. Grease these bolts, both on the threads and under the head, as you fit them, and tighten snugly. If you're riding the bike and the saddle is wobbling about on the post, you'll probably have to replace the whole seatpost – the serrations on the clamp will have lost their bite and won't hold the saddle rails securely. Another issue crops up with posts that are made in two parts. Check for movement between these parts and replace the post if in doubt.

ADJUSTING SADDLE POSITION

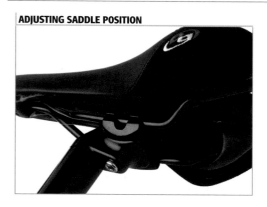

◀ **Step 1:** This is the most common type of saddle fixing. The saddle rails are clamped between two plates with a single bolt. The bottom of the lower plate is curved to match the top of the post. Loosening the bolt (6mm Allen key) allows you to slide the saddle backwards and forwards or to roll it to change the angle. Remove and regrease the fixing bolt regularly.

◀ **Step 2:** This design allows you to control the angle of the saddle precisely. To tip the saddle nose downwards, loosen the back bolt slightly and tighten the front bolt firmly, one turn at a time. To lift the nose, loosen the front bolt one turn and tighten the back bolt. To slide the saddle along on the rails, loosen both bolts equally, reposition the saddle, then retighten the bolts equally.

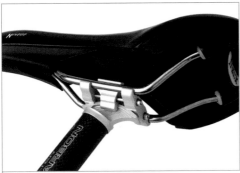

◀ **Step 3:** This design has two small Allen keys at the back of the clamp. Loosen both to slide the saddle rails in the clamp or to roll the clamp over the curved top of the post.

SADDLE ANGLE

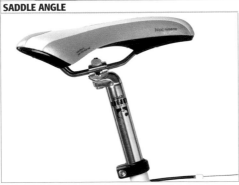

◀ **Step 1:** Saddle angle is critical for a comfortable ride. Pedalling in this position, with the nose of the saddle tipped upwards, will push you off the back of the saddle, lifting the front wheel off the ground when climbing. Your thighs will also get tired with the effort of pulling your body forwards as you push down on the pedals.

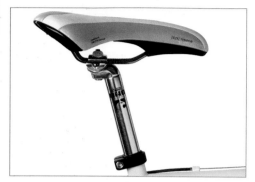

◀ **Step 2:** This position can help relieve the discomfort of a saddle that doesn't suit you, but it tips you forward, towards the bars, causing wrist and shoulder pain. This position is also often a sign that your saddle is too high – try levelling it off and dropping your seatpost a few millimetres into the frame.

◀ **Step 3:** A level saddle position is always the best starting point.

Toolbox

- **Allen keys** – your main tool for adjusting the position of your components will almost always be the humble Allen key. Quality components deserve good-quality tools, cheap Allen keys will round off the heads of bolts, which creates plenty of frustration
- **Grease** – the threads of retaining bolts need a spot of grease to help tighten them firmly and stop them corroding
- **Degreaser** – creaking interfaces will often benefit from being stripped, cleaned and reassembled. If dirt works its way between two clamped surfaces, they'll shift about under pressure

Cleats and pedals: cleats

Cleat positioning is very important. Clamping your feet in one position then pedalling hard for hours can quickly make your knees sore if the position isn't perfect. As a guideline you should position your cleat so the pedal axle sits under the middle of the ball of your foot.

Sit with the backs of your thighs on a table, letting your legs dangle. They probably don't hang straight or at the same angle. Set the angle of the cleats so that your feet are held as close as possible to the natural angle they hang at.

Go for a trial ride with a 4mm Allen key and keep adjusting your angle and position until your feet feel really comfortable and you can clip in and out without your knees hurting. Your shoes shouldn't rub on the cranks as you pedal because you will wear away the metal and create a weak point in the crank – and scuff your shoes.

Arrow

▲ **Arrow pointing forwards, writing facing outwards**

Shimano cleats

Time cleats

Set the release tension in your pedals. It's important that both sides of both pedals have the same tension. The most common adjusting bolt has a 3mm Allen key head. If you're not sure whether both sides of each pedal have equal tension, screw all four (both sides of both pedals) all the way in (clockwise) and then count out the clicks as the bolt turns. Start with the lowest tension that will still retain your feet, tightening gradually as you become confident. Properly adjusted cleats should avoid pain in knees and ankles. If you get sore knees when you cycle with cleats, get a medical opinion on your cleat position. Cycling physiotherapists are very valuable for this; if you find one, nurture him or her.

Eventually your cleats wear out. They start by being hard to clip in. Renew them at this point because they will soon become hard to clip out of. Fresh cleats don't wear the retaining mechanism so fast either. The other type of cleat wear comes from walking on it. Shoes with thick soles hold the cleats clear of the ground, but with thinner soles or worn thicker ones, the bottom of the cleat gets scuffed along the ground. This doesn't harm the cleat until it's worn almost through, but it does wear the heads off the Allen bolts that fix the cleat to the shoe. It's better to keep an eye on them and replace before they become so worn that you have to drill them out.

Check the condition of your cleats regularly, especially if they touch the ground when you walk. The bolts wear down and become difficult to remove. Grease the bolt threads before fitting them and replace the cleats before the Allen key sockets get too worn to accept the key. Scrape out mud and grit before you fit in the key too. If the key sits deep in the hole, it is less likely to slip around it.

Shimano PD-M747

Check pedal bearings by holding the pedal body and twisting it sideways. The pedal should feel firm on the axle and should not knock from side to side. Spin each pedal on its axle. It should turn silently, and keep spinning freely.

If the pedals are knocking or binding, it's new bearing time. They're an unusual size: ³⁄₃₂ inch. If your bike shop doesn't have them, try a bearing shop. If the bearing surfaces or cones are pitted or otherwise damaged, replace the whole axle. Don't swap the plastic sleeves between pedals – I do one pedal at a time to avoid confusion.

This is one of those applications where it makes sense to use a good waterproof grease. Pedals often end up being dragged through puddles, and get stuck in the ground every time you crash. Waterproof grease will hinder the corrosion of the bearing surfaces, as well as saving you precious pedalling energy. There are plenty of good bicycle-specific makes, I generally use Finish Line. A sticky grease helps keep all the balls in place during reassembly as well.

SERVICING THE PEDALS

Remove both pedals from the bike, remembering that the left-hand pedal has a reverse thread and comes off clockwise. The right-hand pedal has a normal thread and comes off anticlockwise.

You'll need a specific pedal spanner for those pedals with spanner flats – they're a standard size, 15mm, but the flats are much narrower than normal.

Once you've got the pedals off, follow the instructions below on how to replace the bearings. The tricky part is the final readjustment – you'll have to reassemble the pedal and refit it before you can be sure that the adjustment is correct. Sometimes it takes a couple of goes – adjusting the pedals, reassembling the pedals and checking the adjustment – before you're satisfied.

SERVICING THE PEDALS

◀ **Step 1:** To strip the pedal you need the Shimano grey plastic pedal tool, which you can order through your bike shop. Clamp the tool in a vice and turn the pedal in the direction of the arrow printed on the tool. Wrap a cloth around the pedal for extra grip if necessary. The threads are plastic and strip if forced backwards, so check the direction carefully.

◀ **Step 2:** Pull the pedal right off the axle. Take the axle out of the vice, remove the plastic tool and clamp the pedal axle back in the vice, narrow end upwards. You see the top row of bearings (A) trapped under the cone. The second set is between the steel tube and the washer below it.

◀ **Step 3:** The top of the pedal has two spanner flats, 7mm and 10mm. Shimano has a neat cone-adjusting tool, which makes the job easier, but you can use ordinary spanners. The 10mm must be narrow to fit in the space. First remove the locknut, then the cone; the lower one is the cone and takes a narrow 10mm spanner, the upper one is the locknut and needs a 7mm spanner.

Cone

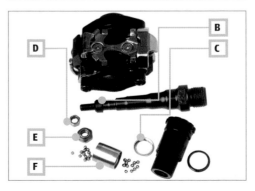

◀ **Step 4:** Remove the lock nut and cone. Pick off all the bearings, then pull off the steel tube and rubber spacer, lift off the lower washer complete with bearings. Pull off the plastic sleeve and the rubber seal. Clean all parts carefully and check for pitted bearing surfaces. If they're worn out, replace the axle. (B) Rubber sleeve; (C) Lower washer; (D) Locknut; (E) Cone; (F) Steel tube.

◀ **Step 5:** Refit rubber seal and plastic sleeve. Grease and refit curved washer. Place 12 $\frac{5}{32}$ inch bearings carefully on the washer, then slide it gently over the axle to rest on top of the plastic sleeve. Refit the rubber spacer. Grease the bearing surface in one end of the metal tube, then pack another 12 bearings onto it. Slide it carefully over the axle.

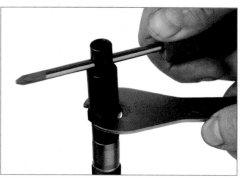

◀ **Step 6:** The adjustment of the cone is crucial. It must be tightened so that there is no play between the axle and the metal tube, but so that the tube can still turn freely. Wind it on by hand, then hold it still while you tighten the locknut down onto it. Test and repeat to find the right adjustment. Refit the axle assembly into the pedal body, then use the grey tool to tighten firmly.

Choosing the right gear

Buying gear and accessories is one of the fun things about owning a bike but choose carefully. You'll find that some buys make a permanent place for themselves in your life, whereas other stuff, which once seemed like a good idea, is more trouble than it's worth.

Liquid

Cycling is hard enough work without being thirsty as well. A litre an hour is often thrown about as a guideline, but you should increase

this in hot weather. Water bottles on your frame are a great low-tech solution, but protect the drinking nozzle if your trails take you through farms – muddy bottles don't bother me, but I don't like the thought of drinking farmyard debris.

Luggage

Most people carry everything on their backs or round their waists. I like to make an exception for tools, which I think are best carried in a seatpack under your saddle. They're usually oily, so you don't want them knocking around in your bag with clothes and sandwiches. And if you fall off, the last thing you want to land on is your toolbag.

For day rides, hydration systems with luggage capacity – as pioneered by CamelBak – are great. If you live somewhere wet make sure you get something waterproof – there is absolutely no point in carrying an extra layer all day then having to wring it out before you put it on. For hot climates concentrate on getting enough air circulating between bag and back to keep you as cool as possible. Larger bags take heavier loads, so look for wider breathable straps. Bags with lots of little pockets are more expensive, but it is worthwhile having different compartments if only so that you can keep your spare socks separate from your sandwiches.

Mudguards

If you live somewhere dry and dusty, skip this section. I do like cycling in all those places that don't have mud, and I agree it can be fun – especially because the weather is usually sunny – but I always worry that it's just not real. So, for real cyclists who get muddy, a word about mudguards.

I think that a front "crudguard", some variation on the theme of a piece of plastic strapped securely to your downtube (or equivalent), is an essential piece of gear. I have eaten too many pieces of tyre-grated cowpat in my life already and if not eating any more comes at the price of fixing an ugly piece of plastic to my bike, it's worth it. The guard also helps to stop bits of stuff from your front tyre getting flicked up into your eyes. Even if you wear glasses the angle of approach from the back of your tyre is perfect to slip lumps of crud under the bottom of your glasses. Strap on a front guard today.

If you can't bear to spend hard-earned cash on a plastic moulding, cut a water-bottle in half, punch some holes in it and ziptie it on. Guards can also make great emergency shovels and, with a good wash, make a lovely camping plate into the bargain.

Back mudguards aren't quite so useful, but if it's cold as well as wet, they make the leap into the essential items basket. I can't bear spray from my back wheel hitting the gap at the top of my jacket collar, trickling cold rain down my back. Again, I will put up with ugly plastic on my bike if it helps keep me warm and dry. And when I get home, I won't give up my place by the fire to a colder person with a prettier bike.

Lights

Night rides are fun. They bring on some kind of ancestral night vision that often let you ride sections faster at night because all the extraneous information your brain normally processes is invisible. I like it best when there's enough moon to see by – otherwise you'll need lights. The faster you go, the more powerful you need your lights to be – you need to be able to see far enough ahead to have time to react to things that appear in your pool of light before you arrive at them. And here's a safety message – don't do anything dangerous. If you can't see there, don't go there!

With lights under 5W in power, you have to move fairly slowly, even if there's a bit of moon. All batteries also contain a heap of environmentally unpleasant stuff and we use far too many of the disposable ones as it is, so treat yourself to at least 10W of rechargeable units. Make sure they're strapped on securely.

Glossary: the language of bikes

From Aheadset to Ziptie, this list covers most of the odd word and phrases that you are going to need in order to talk about bicycles and their mysteries. It's easy to get confused since many of the names that refer to specific parts also have more general meanings. Stick with these definitions and you should be okay.

- **Aheadset:** The bearing that clamps the fork securely to the frame, while allowing the fork to rotate freely so you can steer. The now-standard Aheadset design works by clamping the stem directly to the steerer tube of the forks, allowing you to adjust the bearings by sliding the stem up and down the steerer tube with an Allen key.
- **Air spring:** Used in both suspension forks and shocks, an air spring consists of a sealed chamber pressurized with a pump. The chamber acts as a spring, resisting compression and springing back as soon as any compressing force is released. Air has a natural advantage as a spring medium for bicycles – it's very light.
- **Antiseize:** This compound is spread on the interface of two parts, preventing them sticking together. It is vital on titanium parts, since the metal is very reactive, and will seize happily and permanently on to anything to which it is bolted.
- **Axle:** The axle is the central supporting rod that passes through wheels and bottom brackets and around which they can rotate.
- **Balance screws:** These are found on V-brakes and cantilevers and allow you to alter the preload on the spring that pulls the brake away from the rim so that the two sides of the brake move evenly and touch the rim at the same time.
- **Bar ends:** Handlebar extensions that give you extra leverage when climbing and permit you to use a variety of hand positions for long days out.
- **Barrel-adjuster:** This is a threaded end-stop for the outer casing. Turning the barrel moves the outer casing in its housing, changing the distance the inner cable has

to travel from nipple to cable clamp bolt, and so altering the tension in the cable.
- **Bleeding:** The process of opening the hydraulic brake system, allowing air to escape, and refilling the resulting gap with oil. Bleeding is necessary because, unlike brake fluid, air is compressible. If there's air in your system, pulling the brakes on squashes the air, rather than forcing the brake pads onto the rotors.
- **Bottom bracket cups:** These threaded cups on either side of the bottom bracket bolt on to your frame. The right-hand cup has a reverse thread and is often integral to the main body of the bottom bracket unit.
- **Bottom bracket:** The main bearing connects the cranks through your frame. Often ignored because it's invisible, the smooth running of this part saves you valuable energy.
- **Bottoming-out:** This suspension term means that the fork or shock has completely compressed to the end of its travel. Sometimes accompanied by a loud clunk, bottoming-out is not necessarily a problem – if you don't do it at least once every ride, you're not using the full extent of the travel.
- **Brake arch:** On suspension forks, this is a brace between the two lower legs that passes over the tyre and increases the stiffness of the fork. It is called a brake arch even if your brakes are down by your hub.
- **Brake blocks:** These fit onto your V-brake or cantilever brakes. Pulling the brake cable forces them onto your rim, slowing you down.
- **Brake pads:** On disc brakes, these hard slim pads fit into the disc callipers and are

pushed onto the rotors by pistons inside the brake calliper. They can be cable or hydraulically operated. Being made of very hard material, they last longer than you'd expect for their size, and, unlike V-brake blocks, do not slow you down if they rub slightly against the rotors. Contamination with brake fluid renders them useless instantly.

◆ **Brake pivot:** This is the stud on the frame or forks onto which cantilever or V-brakes bolt. Brakes rotate around the pivot so that the brake blocks hit the rim.

◆ **B-screw:** This component sits behind your derailleur hanger and adjusts its angle. Set too close, the chain rattles on the sprockets; set too far, your shifting is sluggish.

◆ **Burn-in time:** New disc brake pads need burning in; they never brake powerfully fresh from the box. Burn new pads in by braking repeatedly, getting gradually faster, until the brakes bite properly.

◆ **Cable stop:** This part of the frame holds the end of a section of outer casing but allows the cable to pass though it.

◆ **Cable:** This steel wire connects brake and gear levers to shifters and units. It must be kept clean and lubricated for smooth shifting and braking.

◆ **Calliper:** This mechanical or hydraulic disc brake unit sits over the rotor and houses the brake pads.

◆ **Cantilever:** (1) This older rim brake type connects to your brake cable by a second, V-shaped cable; (2) A suspension design that sees the back wheel connected to a swingarm that pivots around a single point. These designs are simple and elegant.

◆ **Cantilever brake:** See cantilever.

◆ **Cartridge bearing:** These sealed bearing units are more expensive than ball bearings, but they are usually better value since the bearing surface is part of the unit, and so is replaced at the same time.

◆ **Casing:** Usually black, this flexible tube supports cables. Brake and gear casings are different: a brake cable has a close spiral winding for maximum strength when compressed; a gear casing has a long spiral winding for maximum signal accuracy.

◆ **Cassette:** This is the cluster of sprockets attached to your back wheel.

◆ **Chain-cleaning box:** This clever device makes chain cleaning less of a messy chore, increasing the chances of you doing it. (Now you just need a chain-cleaning, box-cleaning box.)

◆ **Chainring:** This is one of the rings of teeth your pedals are connected to.

◆ **Chainset:** See crankset.

◆ **Chainsuck:** A bad thing! When your chain doesn't drop neatly off the bottom of the chainring, but gets pulled up and around the back, it jams between chainring and chainstay. Usually caused by worn parts, chainsuck is occasionally completely inexplicable.

◆ **Clamp bolt:** This holds cables in place. There is usually a groove on the component, indicating exactly where the cable should be clamped.

◆ **Cleat:** Bolted to the bottom of your shoe, this metal key-plate locks securely into the pedal and releases instantly when you twist your foot.

◆ **Clipless pedal:** Pedals built around a spring that locks onto a matching cleat on your shoe. It locks you in securely and releases you instantly when you twist your foot.

◆ **Coil spring:** Usually steel but occasionally titanium, coil springs provide a durable, reliable conventional spring in forks and rear shocks.

◆ **Compression damping:** This is the control of the speed at which forks or shock can be compressed.

◆ **Cone:** This curved nut has a smooth track that traps bearings while allowing them to move freely around the axle without leaving any room for side-to-side movement. The amount of space available for the bearings is adjusted by moving the cone along the axle, which is then locked into place with the locknut.

◆ **Crank:** Your pedals bolt onto cranks. The left-hand one has a reverse pedal thread.

◆ **Crank extractor:** This tool removes cranks from axles. There are two different kinds available – one for tapered axles, the other for splined axles.

◆ **Crankset:** The crankset is made up of three chainrings that pull the chain around them when you turn the pedals.

● **Cup-and-cone bearings:** These bearings roll around a cup on either side of the hub, trapped in place by a cone on either side. So that the wheel can turn freely with no side-to-side movement, set the distance between the cones by turning the cones so that they move along the axle threads.

● **Damping:** Damping controls how fast a suspension unit reacts to a force.

● **Derailleur hanger:** The rear derailleur bolts onto this part. This is usually the first casualty of a crash, bending when the rear derailleur hits the ground. Once bent it makes shifting sluggish. Luckily, hangers are quick and easy to replace, but there is no standard size; take your old one when you buy a new one, and get a spare for next time too.

● **Disc brake:** This braking system uses a calliper, mounted next to the front or rear hub, that brakes on a rotor or disc bolted to the hub. Hydraulic versions are very powerful. Using a separate braking surface also means the rim isn't worn out with the brake pads.

● **Dish:** Rims need to be adjusted to sit directly in the centreline of your frame, between the outer faces of the axle locknuts. Adding cassettes or discs to one side or other of the hub means the rim needs to be tensioned more on one side than the other to make room for the extra parts.

● **Dishing tool:** This tool allows you to test the position of the rim relative to the end of the axle on either side of the hub.

● **DOT fluid:** The fluid used in DOT hydraulic brakes. Higher numbers – i.e., 5.1 rather than 4.0 – have higher boiling temperatures.

● **Drivetrain:** This is a collective name for all the transmission components: chain, derailleurs, shifters, cassette and chainset.

● **Duct tape:** Like the Force, it has a dark side and a light side, and it holds together the fabric of the universe.

● **Elastomers:** This simple spring medium is usually found only in cheap forks now.

● **End cap (cable end cap):** This is crushed onto the ends of cables to prevent them from fraying and stabbing you when you adjust them.

● **End-stop screw:** Used on derailleurs, this part limits the travel of the derailleurs, preventing them from dropping the chain off either side of the cassette or chainset.

● **Eye bolt:** On cantilever brakes, the stud of the brake block passes through the eye of the bolt. Tightening the nut on the back of the bolt wedges the stud against a curved washer, holding the brake block firmly in place.

● **Ferrule:** This protective end cap for outer casing supports it where it fits into barrel-adjusters or cable stops.

● **Freehub:** This ratcheting mechanism allows the back wheel to freewheel when you stop pedalling. It's bolted to the back wheel, and has splines on to which the cassette slides. This is the part that makes the evocative "tick tick tick" as you cycle along.

● **Freewheel:** This older version of the sprocket cluster on the back wheel combines the sprockets and ratcheting mechanism in one unit. Freewheels are rarely used for multispeed bikes now; the cassette/freehub set-up is far stronger as it supports the bearings nearer the ends of the axle. Freewheels are often found on singlespeed bikes.

● **Front derailleur:** This part moves the chain between the chainrings on your chainset.

● **Gear ratio:** Calculated by dividing chainring size by sprocket size and multiplying by wheel size in inches, the gear ratio determines the number of times your back wheel turns with one revolution of the pedal.

● **Guide jockey:** The upper of the two jockey wheels on the rear derailleur, this part does the actual derailing, guiding the chain from one sprocket to the next as the derailleur cage moves across beneath the cassette.

● **Hop:** This term describes a section of the rim where the spokes don't have enough tension and bulge out further from the hub than the rest of the rim.

● **Hydraulic brakes:** Usually disc brakes, these use hydraulic fluid to push pistons inside the brake calliper against a rotor on the hub. Because brake fluid compresses little under pressure, all movement at the brake lever is accurately transmitted to the calliper.

- **Indexing:** The process of setting up the tension in gear cables so shifter click moves the chain across neatly to the next sprocket or chainring.
- **Instruction manuals:** Often ignored or thrown out, these contain vital information. Keep them and refer to them!
- **International Standard:** This term refers to both rotor fitting and calliper fitting. International Standard rotors and hubs have six bolts. International Standard callipers are fixed to the bike with bolts that point across the frame, not along it.
- **ISIS:** This is a standard for bottom brackets and chainsets and has 10 evenly spaced splines.
- **Jockey wheel:** These small black-toothed wheels route the chain around the derailleur.
- **Lacing:** This technique is used to weave spokes to connect the hub to the rim. This part of wheelbuilding looks difficult, but it is easy once you know how.
- **Link wire:** Used in cantilever brakes, this connects the pair of brake shoes to the brake cable. It is designed to be failsafe; if the brake cable snaps, the link wire falls off harmlessly rather than jamming in the tyre lugs and locking your wheel. You are still left with no brake though...
- **Lockring:** Used on bottom brackets and barrel-adjusters, this is turned to wedge against frame or brake lever to stop the adjustment you've made from rattling loose.
- **Lower legs:** The lower parts of suspension forks, these attach to brake and wheel.
- **Mineral oil:** This hydraulic brake fluid is similar to DOT fluid and must only be used with systems designed for mineral oil. It is greener than DOT, and less corrosive.
- **Modulation:** This is the ratio between brake lever movement and brake pad movement, or how your brake actually feels.
- **Needle bearing:** Similar to a ball bearing, a needle bearing is in the shape of a thin rod rather than a ball. Since there is more contact area between bearing and bearing surface than with the ball type, they are supposed to last longer, but they can be tricky to adjust. They are usually found in headsets, although some very nice bottom brackets also use needle bearings.

- **Nest:** This hanger or stop in a brake lever or gear shifter holds the nipple on the end of the brake or gear cable.
- **Nipple:** (1) This blob of metal at the end of a cable stops it slipping through the nest; (2) This nut on the end of a spoke secures it to the rim and allows you to adjust the spoke tension; (3) This perfectly ordinary part of a bicycle causes the pimply youth in the bike shop to blush furiously when asked for it by women.
- **Noodle:** This short metal tube guides the end of brake cable into V-brake hanger.
- **Octalink:** This is the name of the Shimano eight-splined bottom bracket/chainset fitting.
- **One-key release:** The combination of axle bolt and special washer fits permanently to the bike and doubles as a crank extractor.
- **Pawl:** This part allows you to freewheel: a sprung lever inside ratcheting mechanism in the rear hub is flicked out of the way when the ratchet moves one way, and catches on the ratchet teeth the other way.
- **Pinch bolt:** In this version of a clamp bolt, the cable passes through a hole in the middle of the bolt, rather than under a washer beside the bolt. Occasionally it is found on cantilever straddle hangers.
- **Pinch puncture:** This happens when the tyre hits an edge hard enough to squash the tube on the tyre or rim and puncture it. It is also known as snakebite flat because it makes two neat vertical holes a rim's width apart. Apparently this is what a snake bite looks like, although I've never had a problem with snakes biting my inner tubes.
- **Pivot:** (1) This bearing on a suspension frame allows one part of the frame to move against another; (2) This is also a rod or a bearing around which part of a component rotates.
- **Post mount:** Brake callipers are mounted with bolts that point along the frame, rather than across. These are less common than the alternative, the International Standard mount, but easier to adjust.
- **Preload:** This initial adjustment made to suspension springs to tune forks or shock to your weight is usually made by tweaking the preload adjustment knob, or by adding or removing air from air springs.

◆ **Presta valve:** Also known as high pressure valves, these are more reliable than Schraeder valves, which are designed for lower pressure car and motorcycle tyres. Their only disadvantage is that they cannot be inflated at gas stations.

◆ **Rapid-rise (low-normal):** In this rear derailleur, the cable pulls the chain from larger to smaller sprockets, then, when cable tension is released, the spring pulls the chain back from smaller to larger sprocket.

◆ **Rear derailleur:** This mechanism is attached to the frame on the right-hand side of the rear wheel. It moves the chain from one sprocket to the next, changing the gear ratio, when you move the shifter on your handlebars. It makes odd grinding noises when not adjusted properly.

◆ **Rebound damping:** Rebound damping controls the speed at which the fork or shock re-extends after being compressed.

◆ **Reservoir:** This reserve pool of hydraulic damping fluid is housed in a chamber at the brake lever. Having this reservoir of cool fluid a distance away from the hot rotor and calliper, helps to minimize fluid expansion under heavy braking.

◆ **Reverse thread:** The spiral of the thread runs the opposite way to normal: clockwise for undoing; counterclockwise for tightening.

◆ **Rotor:** Bolted to the hub, this is the braking surface of a disc brake.

◆ **Sag:** This is the amount of travel you use sitting normally on your bike. Setting up suspension with sag gives a reserve of travel above the neutral position.

◆ **Schraeder valve:** This is a fat, car-type valve. The inventor, Franz Schraeder, is buried in a magical spot at the Cirque de Gavarne in the French Pyrenees.

◆ **Seal:** A seal prevents dirt, mud and dust from creeping into the parts of hubs, suspension units, headsets, bottom brackets and any other components where the preferred lubricant is grease rather than mud.

◆ **Seatpost clamp:** These plates and bolts connect the seatpost firmly to your saddle.

◆ **Shim:** This thin piece of metal is used to make two parts fit together precisely. The washers between IS (International Standard) callipers and the frame are shims because they hold the calliper precisely in position.

◆ **Shimano joining pin:** Once split, Shimano chains must only be joined with the correct joining pin. Attempting to rejoin the chain using the original rivet will damage the chain plates.

◆ **Singlespeed (1x1):** This state of peace is obtained through self-liberation from the complexities of modern life by throwing away your gears.

◆ **Snakebite flat:** *See* pinch puncture.

◆ **Socket:** Shaped like a cup, this spanner holds the bolt securely on all the flats.

◆ **Splines:** These ridges across a tool or component are designed to mesh with a matching part so that the two parts turn together.

◆ **Split link:** This chain link can be split and rejoined by hand without damaging the adjacent links.

◆ **Sprocket:** This toothed ring meshes with the chain to rotate the rear wheel. The cassette consists of a row of different-sized sprockets.

◆ **Stanchions:** This upper part of the suspension forks slides into the lower legs and contains all the suspension extras, including springs, damping rods and oil.

◆ **Standard tube:** For those who don't need tubelessness, this normal inner tube is designed to fit into a normal tyre.

◆ **Star fanged nut (star nut, star-fangled nut):** This nut is pressed into the top of the steerer tube. The top cap bolt threads into it, pushing down on the stem and pulling up on the steerer tube.

◆ **Stationary pad:** In disc brakes with one piston, the piston pushes a pad against the rotor, which in turn pushes the rotor against the stationary pad, trapping the rotor between moving and stationary pads.

◆ **Steerer tube:** This single tube extends from the top of the forks through the frame and has the stem bolted on the top.

◆ **Stiff link:** The plates of the chain are squashed too closely together to pass smoothly over the sprockets, and they jump across teeth rather than mesh with the valleys between teeth.

- **Straddle wire:** This connects the two units of a cantilever brake via a straddle hanger on the brake cable.
- **Stress relief:** You can achieve this by squeezing the spokes to settle them into place as you build a wheel.
- **Swingarm:** This is the rear of a suspension frame, to which the back wheel attaches.
- **Tension jockey:** The lower of the two jockey wheels on the rear derailleur is sprung so it constantly pushes backwards, taking up slack in the chain created by the different teeth size combinations of sprockets and chainrings.
- **Toe-clips:** These survive today only in ghost form as the missing clip in clipless pedals. An unfortunate loss is the accompanying toe-strap, which was occasionally a priceless emergency item. (*See* ziptie.)
- **Toe-in:** To prevent squeaking, rim brakes are set up so the front of the brake block touches momentarily earlier than the back.
- **Top cap:** This disc, on the top of your stem, is bolted into the star-fanged nut in the steerer tube. Provided the stem bolts are loose, adjusting the top cap pushes the stem down the steerer tube, tightening the headset bearings. Always retighten the stem afterwards!
- **Travel:** Travel is the total amount of movement in the fork or shock. The longer the travel, the heavier and beefier the fork or shock must be.
- **Triggershifters:** This gear shifter features a pair of levers; one pulling, the other releasing, the cable.
- **Truing wheels:** The process of adjusting the tension in each spoke prevents the rim from wobbling from side to side when the wheel spins.
- **Tubeless:** In this weight-saving tyre design, the bead of the tyre locks into the rim, creating an airtight seal that needs no inner tube.
- **Twistshifters:** These gear shifters work by twisting the handlebar grip. Turning one way pulls through cable, while turning the other way releases cable.
- **Tyre boot:** Stuck onto the inside of a tyre, this patch prevents the inner tube from bulging out of big gashes.
- **URT:** Unified Rear Triangle. In this suspension frame design, bottom bracket, chainset and front derailleur are located together on the swingarm (rear end of the bike), so the movement of the swingarm never affects the length of the chain.
- **UST:** Universal Standard for Tubeless. This is an agreed standard for the exact shape of rims and tyre beads. UST tyres and rims made by different manufacturers lock together neatly for an airtight seal.
- **V-brake:** In these rim brakes, two vertical (hence "V") units connected by the brake cable, hold the blocks.
- **Virtual pivot:** In suspension, this is when the swingarm is made of a series of linkages that combine to rotate around a position. Rather than a physical location on the frame, this position may be a point around which the frame would rotate if it was a simple swingarm.
- **Wheel jig:** This frame for holding a wheel during truing has adjustable indicators that can be set close to the rim to allow you to estimate how round and straight the rim is.
- **Ziptie:** The tool for whenever you need to connect one thing to another.

Index

Page numbers in **bold** refer to illustrations or photographs